Dog Training
BASICS

Miriam Fields-Babineau

Sterling Publishing Co., Inc.
New York

For my parents and grandparents

ACKNOWLEDGMENTS

I want to thank all my clients and their pets who taught me how to be patient and persistent in order to achieve their goals. I also want to thank all those who helped me put together the photographs—my clients, and most of all my friend and neighbor Maria Morrison, who graciously gave of her time and camera. I also want to thank all my dog models: Sydney, Phantom, Mosby, Cherry, Sparky, Beau, Alphie, Teddy, Probie, Marcinko, Thumblina, Shannon, and others that took part. All were great to work with.

Library of Congress Cataloging-in-Publication Data
Fields-Babineau, Miriam.
    Dog training basics / Miriam Fields-Babineau.
        p. cm.
    Includes bibliographical references (p.   ).
    ISBN 0-8069-9406-1
    1. Dogs—Training. I. Title.
SF431.F54 1997
636.7'0887—dc20   96-35793
                                                    CIP

Edited and designed by Rodman Pilgrim Neumann

1 3 5 7 9 10 8 6 4 2

Published by Sterling Publishing Company, Inc.
387 Park Avenue South, New York, N.Y. 10016
© 1997 by Miriam Fields-Babineau
Distributed in Canada by Sterling Publishing
℅ Canadian Manda Group, One Atlantic Avenue, Suite 105
Toronto, Ontario, Canada M6K 3E7
Distributed in Great Britain and Europe by Cassell PLC
Wellington House, 125 Strand, London WC2R 0BB, England
Distributed in Australia by Capricorn Link (Australia) Pty Ltd.
P.O. Box 6651, Baulkham Hills, Business Centre, NSW 2153, Australia
Printed in China

Sterling ISBN 0-8069-9406-1

Contents

Preface

THE MOST IMPORTANT thing I want you to gain from this guide is how to be clear when communicating with a dog, helping it to understand its environment and be happy. Many people, however, will pick up a book on dog training expecting to be able to train their dog just by reading through the book.

Unfortunately, many books simply confuse the dog owner by not giving a starting point, as well as not being clear about what is first, second, and so on in the process of training. It is very difficult for a novice dog owner to pick up the important points of training when the presentation does not follow a logic that is clear and sequential. This guide is carefully designed in a step-by-step progression that reflects the natural process of training a dog. As well, I feel it is important for the dog owner to understand the behavior behind his dog's actions, and then to be able to train his dog with as little confusion as possible.

Almost any animal will respond to food rewards, but you may run into the problem of not always being able to stuff your pockets with treats. Who

Take time to play with your pet. It will relax and rejuvenate both of you.

wants to go to work or school with a pocket full of treats? What if, someday, you forget to stock up on treats, and you require your dog to do something for you? The dog will not respond without its reward in sight, or it may that one time, but if it does not get its customary treat, it likely won't do it again.

Another problem that you may run into is that when your dog is intensely involved in an activity and doesn't see your reward, he simply will not listen to you. While using treats may enable you to get your puppy started on attentiveness, it is highly unreliable and does not teach your dog to respect you.

While toys are highly motivating to some dogs, we again may face the problem of their not paying attention when distracted. It may also become a problem that you must carry the toy with you to get your dog to be attentive to your commands.

All dogs, however, respond to praise, especially from someone they love. I encourage you to use praise at any time *for any reason*. You don't need to stock up on praise, or to show it physically. You need only open your mouth and sound happy and exuberant when your dog does something correctly, encouraging him to continue. Dogs will work hard for simple praise from their owners.

Many have long underrated the intelligence, reasoning abilities, and use of memory of which dogs are capable. An untrained dog is simply ignorant, not at all stupid, until taught about how to interact in its environment. The more training a dog receives, the more intelligence and personality it displays.

In order to train any dog, you must form a communication link between yourself and the canine. Dogs require simple and clear language to understand your desires. You must continue using this language consistently for the rest of your dog's life.

To understand this concept, think of yourself in a foreign country where you do not understand the language or customs of the residents. Trying to do even simple things such as eating or finding a certain place can be very frustrating. Living in this strange environment for a long time without the help of someone teaching the language can cause severe psychological problems.

Now, think of the bored dog who chews on household items, turns over the garbage can, or digs up the yard. It indicates the absence of proper teaching; this dog does not understand the limitations of its environment, nor what is right in order to please its owner. Would you let your children destroy household items? No, you would be sure that they

Three dogs performing the sit/stay together.

knew the difference between right and wrong. You would teach them this through words, intonation, and, sometimes perhaps, physical reprimand. Your child learns your wishes through your consistent use of repeated words.

Your child goes to school! Why not your dog? You should think of your dog as an eternal child, never growing up and moving away. Your dog will be dependent on you throughout its life, counting on you for food, shelter, knowledge, and love.

As any parent knows, the younger the child, the more patience is necessary to obtain the proper responses. This is also true of dogs. Although a puppy requires more patience in training than does an older dog, it will also show better retention of what is learned. Therefore, the earlier you begin training, the greater the rewards will be.

I prefer to begin a dog's training process as early as eight weeks. This may be difficult for the average puppy owner, for it requires endless amounts of patience, but the rewards will be tremendous. Doing this will prevent many future behavior problems, making the dog's adolescent period (five to nine months) easier to deal with.

Nevertheless, a dog is never too old to learn obedience. As long as you remain consistent, your dog will respond correctly. Most dogs, no matter how old, thoroughly enjoy working, for they become the center of attention, and are very happy to be learning how to please you. It gives them an occupation—something to look forward to and strive for, to receive your adoration for.

If you intend to have a dog just for the sake of having a pet, think again. A dog is an intelligent animal that needs to be developed. It needs to become a part of the family, not to be a forgotten item left outside and ignored. The Monks of New Skete have a good solution to this dilemma. Instead of buying a dog, they get a goat or donkey. Like people, dogs are social animals, requiring both stimulation and communication to be happy.

Sydney and Miriam during the filming of a Chevrolet commercial. This requires complete distraction-proofing. The dog must be oblivious to everything going on around her and maintain her attention on her trainer.

I have written this book to give you a better understanding of your canine friend. I will show you how to communicate with each other, and, most of all, how to live a happy, harmonious life together.

Owning a dog should be a pleasurable experience. By following my instructions carefully and consistently, you will create a true relationship between you and the canine in your life.

Miriam Fields-Babineau

PRETRAINING

1. Why Train?

Have you ever been to a zoo and seen the caged animals pacing inside their enclosures or making strange movements with their bodies?

If so, you have seen a variety of psychoses and neuroses developed over a long period of forced inactivity. These abnormal behaviors occupy the animals' time, for there is nothing else they can do.

The zoo provides these animals with food and shelter, effectively eliminating their primary activity and purpose in their native habitat. In captivity, these animals no longer have an occupation. They soon become lethargic and apathetic, developing both physical and mental irregularities. They no longer digest their food properly, reproduce normally, or care for their own coats.

Over the years, much of my work has been assisting zoos in developing training procedures to provide animals with an occupation, a purpose in life. These projects have been very successful with several species. As a result, many other zoos have adopted similar training procedures. The training provides a means where by animals must work for their food, just as they would in the wild. The animals that underwent the training have shown a considerable improvement in their reproduction and acceptance of life in captivity. They began to care for their coats, digest their food properly, and stop their unusual pacing, among other things. It is through proper training that they have learned to understand their environment.

A domestic animal, such as a dog, is actually a captive animal. It cannot wander as it pleases, and does not have to spend its time seeking food and shelter. You, as a caring and adoring owner, provide for all of your animal's needs. This leaves your pet to provide for his own entertainment.

What would any normal person do in captivity with nothing to do? Go crazy with boredom! The same is true of your dog. The entertainment your dog chooses can sometimes take the form of what we call bad habits—usually destructive. After all, your dog was only trying to find something to occupy himself while you were busy or gone.

Almost every breed of dog originates from selective breeding for specific characteristics to perform a particular job, some for hunting, others for guarding and herding. Without performing these instinctual tasks on a regular basis your pet will begin to develop anxiety. The anxiety brings on psychoses and neuroses as it does to the animals at a zoo.

Training your dog gives him an occupation—something to think about, look forward to, and expand his intellectual abilities—and produces understanding and discipline. Dogs appreciate structure and consistency, helping them relax in their captive environments.

The most important aspect of training is learning to communicate with each other—dog owner and dog. In this manner your dog learns what you desire from him, fulfilling his life by allowing him to show his loyalty and love for you in the only way he knows: by pleasing you.

This understanding between you and your pet is very important for a well-adjusted animal. When your dog understands the household standards and limitations, he will follow these rules simply to keep you happy.

If your dog regresses and breaks a rule, such as chewing a table leg or messing on the carpet, you should be able to recognize immediately why it happened. Although this requires time and patience, training your pet enables you to learn how to recognize the reasoning behind the "accident." For example, if your pet messes on the carpet, there are several questions you can ask yourself to find the root of the problem and solve it there, instead of constantly miscommunicating with your pet. Was the dog fully housebroken to begin with, or does he have occasional accidents? Is there some form of new stress in your or your pet's life? Did you remember to stick to the "potty" schedule?

Many dogs will protest new variations in diet, environment, and schedules.

Remember: Dogs Are Creatures of Habit.

While you train your dog, you will learn to recognize all his behaviors and the reason for them. This will ensure your developing an understanding, harmonious relationship.

Keep in mind your dog cannot possibly understand your complex language. Canines communicate on a more basic, simple level. Thus, when you are going into a detailed explanation of why Foofoo shouldn't have messed the carpet—and he sits there cocking his head from side to side—it is not a sign of understanding, but one of incomprehension or confusion. If your pet understood you, he would be looking you straight in the face with a peaceful expression.

With time, patience, and consistency *you* can learn.

There is never an excuse for failing to train your dog, no matter what his age or physical condition. While an older dog may not accept or retain the learning as well as a young puppy, he will still enjoy the interaction with you that training provides. This includes the deaf, blind, aged, three-legged, stubborn, and especially obedience school dropouts. They are all willing and able to learn.

The old adage that you can't teach an old dog new tricks pertains more to stubborn *people* than to older canines.

2. Dog Think!

TO PROPERLY TRAIN a dog, you must understand how he thinks and communicates. Dogs have several means of communication. They use different methods depending on whether they are socializing with their own species or with another. If they are communicating with other dogs, they use body language, vocal tones, and scent.

Dogs have a distinct social order within their own packs or families. The dominant dog—the alpha—is usually the oldest and/or the strongest. Training a highly dominant dog can be more difficult, for he will feel displaced from his social structure and continue to vie for the most dominant position. With these dogs, it is important to be more persistent and to refrain from showing signs of hesitation or of giving in, which might contribute to the dog's developing behaviors that become bad habits.

If your dog attempts dominance over you by stubbornly continuing to mess in the house, growl, snap, sit on you, or not allow you to take things from his mouth, then I recommend that you consult a professional trainer to correct the problem.

The dog can only communicate effectively with humans with body language. Dogs often try to communicate vocally, but fail to get the point across to

Attentive expression. Beau, a Beagle, is watching his trainer.

the human listener due to the inability of humans to recognize the differences in the dog's pitch and frequency.

A person who has owned a dog for some time may be able to distinguish some different tones as anxious, frustrated, or displeased. Normally, you will not have to perceive these auditory signals in order to train your dog properly. However, as you spend more time with your dog, you may find that you can recognize these behaviors more easily.

It is very important to learn to "read" your dog. A dog speaks through his eyes, facial expressions, body positions, and, particularly, his ears. As you observe your puppy in play, note his expressions. Every dog has a variety of different expressions. The only way to learn to read your dog is by careful close observation as the dog is involved in various activities.

Learning to read your dog is an important start for basic obedience training. For example, you will need to know whether your sniffing dog needs to relieve himself or is just interested in exploring his territory. From the sounds that he is making, you must be able to determine whether he is actually hurt or merely frustrated. You must learn whether your dog is tired or, perhaps, just being lazy.

Understanding these differences will have a tremendous effect on your dog's training progress. If your dog is tired and you force him to continue working, you may inadvertently affect him adversely so that he develops a negative association that he will then bring to any future training sessions.

Think about the understanding a mother has for her infant. To anyone other than the infant's parents, the baby might seem to cry whenever it wants something, or simply without reason. The mother, however, always knows what her baby wants. She has learned through observation and the trial-and-error process. Developing such an understanding is much the same with your dog.

In learning to read your dog, take the example of a dog "smiling": The ears lie flat back, the tail is either wagging in a low position or held between the legs, and the gums are drawn away from the teeth, showing both their front and sides. Many people would think this expression was threatening. It is just the opposite! A dog "smiling" at you in this manner is showing complete submission, as he greets you.

There are seven main body positions that you should be aware of.

Body Language

1. Overt Aggression—The overt aggressor may attack unprovoked. The dog makes itself look as big as possible. The fur along his neck and spine will stand straight up, along with the tail. His ears are perked forward, neck stretched forward and up,

Waiting for a command.

and legs stiff. His eyes will connect with those of his challenger. His lips will be drawn back from the sides of his jaw, showing his large incisors and sharp molars.

2. Fear Aggression—This dog will only attack if he feels threatened. He holds his tail between the legs of his hunched body, holding his shoulders lower than his rear, his neck stretched out and held below his shoulders. The fur will stand up along the back of his neck and on his rear. His ears will be flat against his head as his eyes stare at the source of the fear. The sides of his lips will quiver and may show his incisor teeth.

3. Alert—The body will be still, with the head up and tail held straight out. The dog will be staring at the source of his reaction as his ears swivel to pick up the sounds. Some dogs will raise the fur on the back of their necks.

Alert posture. Toby, a Catahoula Leopard, sees something in the distance.

Phantom, a White Shepherd, is wearing a Halti head collar, attentively awaiting his next command.

Sydney, an Australian Shepherd, is demonstrating the body language of a happy, relaxed dog.

4. **Passive/Relaxed**—The dog's tail is down, his head moves around freely, with no eye contact, his ears take in the surrounding sounds but do not zero in, and he will usually pant. The most relaxed position will be lying down.

5. **Invitation to Play**—Many dogs will bounce around, jump, and roll. It may be difficult to tell the difference between a dog inviting play, and one demanding it. The "demander" will tend to bark loudly and attain eye contact as he assumes

Sydney shows a combined expression of relaxation, attentiveness, and enjoyment.

Invitation to play. The front of the dog is down, with the hind end raised. If the dog has a tail, it will be wagging from side to side. Some dogs will bark excitedly when they assume this position.

the play position. The "requester" will pant and not attain eye contact. The dog will keep his hind end up, tail high and wagging, hold his front end down with the forelegs spread and facing forward. His ears will be forward or sideways.

6. **Active Submission**—This is mostly seen when a dog greets someone he perceives as authoritative (or alpha). It is also noticeable when you are punishing your pet. The dog will crouch low to the ground, tail held low, ears flat, eyes blinking, nose up. Some dogs will "smile," wrinkle their noses, and clack their teeth. Others will lift a forepaw.

7. **Passive Submission**—A very submissive dog will display this position if he is afraid or intimidated. The dog lies on its back, showing his stomach. His head will be laid back and off to the side, with his mouth closed and his eyes closed or blinking. His tail will be between his widespread legs, and he may urinate.

Charlotte, a young Golden Retriever, is displaying active submission.

Passive submission.

In the wild, several different species of animal group together for protection from predators. It is common to see giraffes feeding with antelopes and baboons in the same area. These animals utilize different parts of the same environment and also provide mutual protection from predators. The language they use must be completely understood by all the species. Therefore, all body movements have meaning, such as signifying distress or alarm. If an animal is frightened, another animal will smell the fright through chemical reception (olfactory communication), coupled with the vocal cry of alarm. The first animals to react begin a chain reaction within the herds, and on to the other species surrounding them.

The canine, usually the predator, will recognize when its prey has knowledge of its presence. This recognition is through the scent, sound, and movements of the prey. Dogs have a sophisticated means of communication with their pack members that aids in their hunting skills. Again, using their senses of scent, sound, and sight, they will place themselves in the appropriate areas (according to dominance hierarchy) in order to make an efficient kill. A pack of dogs will always surround first, and then they will attack from all sides.

It is important to understand your dog's different modes of communication with all types of other animals as well as with people. This is all part of learning to communicate with him. Observing your pet in different activities, such as play, greeting, and working, will aid in a more thorough understanding of his personality.

If your dog is friendly, he will ordinarily be subordinate to another dog upon greeting. For example, he will allow sniffing of his face and anal region, may lie down in a passive submission position, or simply sit, allowing a completion of the greeting and then running off to play.

This type of dog is very easy to train and will be accepting of your dominance. Be careful, however, to be coercive rather than forceful when training, or you may intimidate him.

Dogs play roughly. They'll bite, tumble, and jump.

Many dogs, male and female, will "mount" another dog. Some of these canines will also attempt this with their owners. This is not a sexual behavior, but rather a hierarchy challenge: a clear sign of a dominant animal. He will display dominant behavior while playing with other dogs, or with his owner, by pushing the other aside, urinating on him, or mounting.

If your dog displays any of these dominant behaviors, be sure to be extremely consistent when training him. Do not give him a single inch! He will constantly be testing and challenging, so never give in to it. You cannot let such a dog think he can take advantage of you in any situation.

If your dog growls upon meeting another dog, remove him from the area immediately. He must learn some basic obedience so that you can control him in a distraction situation. When he is under control, then you can gradually add other animals as he learns to become sociable.

If you see your puppy showing dominant behavior, be sure to address the problem while he is young; otherwise you will have to deal with an aggressive dog when he reaches adulthood.

I have seen numerous dogs run a household by inspiring fear in their owners. They can sometimes be very loving dogs, but if they are not given their own way, they may growl at or even bite their owners. By the time the behavior has gone this far, the owner may be too afraid to reprimand the dog, causing the problem to become worse.

Stress yawn. Do, a Dalmatian, wants to go play.

Although you may think feisty behavior is "cute" in your puppy, think again. Is it cute when you or your child is bitten with the puppy's sharp teeth? Even puppies can cause serious damage if the behavior is not corrected. A bite can cause a child serious trauma, resulting in an overall fear of dogs.

People and Dogs

The body language a dog uses with you depends on how you are communicating with your own body and scent. Dogs can perceive every mood you are experiencing. Therefore, it is important that you focus your attention on him during every training session. If you are distracted, your dog will immediately know it, and take advantage of the moment. For example, you put your dog in a sit/stay, and get into a conversation with a neighbor. Next thing you know, your dog is up walking around or pulling on the lead to go say "Hello" to another dog. He knew you weren't paying attention, and took advantage. Your eyes left him, your voice was not directed to him, and your scent denoted your inattentiveness.

Knowing how your entire body communicates with your pet will help you maintain consistency during the initial training stages. You must be able to recognize signs of disobedience and regression, or you will lose ground with your dog, and have to retrain. Remember, you are your dog's leader. He will experience the same emotions and reactions as you.

Attentive posture. Cassie, a Miniature Poodle, is enjoying her training session, performing with a smile.

Dogs go through different stages in life just as people do. As young puppies between the ages of two and four months they will remain close, due to their insecurity. They are also at their peak learning time, their minds like sponges, soaking up all their experiences. This is the best training time!

When your dog reaches the age of five months, adolescence begins. This period lasts until the dog reaches nine months. By this time his teeth are all in, and the testing of his environment is reduced. This period is the most difficult time to train a pet. The dog is re-bellious, independent, and trying to place himself at the top of the hierarchy. If you are beginning to work with your dog at this age, be certain to be firm, consistent, and patient. Remember, it is only a phase. Your dog will turn out fine when his hormones settle down, by about ten months of age.

No matter what the age of your pet, he can have bad days, just like many people. We can't all be on top of our game every day, so don't expect your pet to be, either. There are, however, several periods during training when the bad days occur with the most frequency. This "learning plateau" normally happens first at the time you teach him the down/stay, and then again midway through the off-lead work. You may find that your dog is behaving as if he'd never learned the meaning of "Heel," "Sit," or "Stay" and he may even regress on housebreaking.

Do not give up on your dog in frustration. Make sure he follows through with all commands through persistence and patience. As long as you remain consistent he will learn he must listen, relax, and behave. Never end a training session on a bad note. Make sure your dog follows at least one command correctly before stopping.

Children and Dogs

There is nothing more exciting to a child than getting its first puppy. During the first couple of weeks the child will want to help care for him. Unfortunately the novelty wears off and you will find yourself reminding your child to feed or take the puppy outside. Then it becomes a chore.

Thumblina, an Old English Sheepdog, is heeling with Kyle, a ten-year-old.

Regardless of your having gotten the dog for the children, the responsibility falls on you to train and care for your new family member. Don't expect your children to be able to follow a consistent regimen. Their lives are fraught with inconsistencies and erratic changes. Dogs require structure. Without it, they will have a great deal of anxiety that may lead to various behavior problems.

The best means of getting your children involved with your dog is to first train the canine, and then teach the children how to work with him. All children over the age of five can learn how to interact and say the appropriate words if they are properly guided and observed.

The burden now falls on you. You will have to remind yourself why you got the dog in the first place. Was it because you wanted your child to have a pet, and learn responsibility? Sure, that was the original reason, but now you find you simply added another child to your household. The main difference between the human and the canine is that the canine will never grow up.

Dogs remain children forever. Although they will go through various stages during puppyhood, and they do eventually mature into adult dogs, they will never "grow up" and move out. Throughout their lives they will look for ways to challenge you, much the same as a child.

Children over ten years old can learn how to do leash work with their dog. It is still important, however, to make sure the dog knows what he is doing before the child is on the other end of the leash. A child will need to concentrate on handling the dog, and will quickly become frustrated if the dog is jumping all over and biting the leash.

A child over twelve years old may be able to learn how to train a dog as well as handle it. Keep in mind, however, that children of this age are still easily distracted, which can cause some confusion for your pet. If you want your child to train the dog, observe the training sessions, so you can remind your child to pay attention, or make sure of consistency.

Even if your children are teenagers you cannot leave the responsibility of the dog totally in their hands. Teenagers have a lot on their minds, from friends, school, and the opposite sex to the pressures of the world. Unfortunately, a pet will slip by the wayside.

Remember, it is your responsibility to care for and train your new dog!

Child's Fear of Dogs

Many children have had the misfortune of a bad experience involving a dog. While there may be some who heal quickly—usually those who already own a dog—there are others who may well develop a phobia.

A child who is afraid may become terrified at the mere sight of a dog. Some parents will inadvertently encourage this behavior either by over-coddling and displaying fear also, or by quickly leaving the area. Most children who are afraid may subconsciously feel powerless when confronted with something out of the past that caused pain.

Whether being bitten, being barked at, or the mere presence of a canine was the original cause, you will need to address the phobia.

As with any phobia, you will need to handle this "head-on." There is proven empirical evidence that children raised with pets in the home grow up to become better adjusted, more responsible adults.

Kyle telling Thumblina to stay. He places his visual signal in front of her face as he gives the vocal command.

Your child will need to learn that not all dogs want to inflict fear and pain. Once this is accomplished, the child will feel more in control of his/her own life.

To overcome this problem you need to begin with a well-behaved, trained dog. Expose the fearful child to the animal in the presence of another child of the same age who is not afraid to interact with the dog. The fearful child will see the interaction and begin to feel less threatened by the animal.

The next step is to place the dog in a down/stay. Let the fearful child come and pet it. Keep the dog's head away from the child's hand, as the child touches its back. Once the child isn't afraid to touch the dog, try the same thing with the dog in a sit/stay. If the dog is gentle in taking treats from your hand, have the unfearful child feed him treats, as the fearful child watches.

Eventually, the fearful child will see how much fun the other child is having, and he or she will also want to give the dog a treat. Once the fearful child is able to pet and feed treats to the dog, he/she is then ready to learn how to work with the dog. When he/she begins working with the dog and sees that it responds to commands, the fear will begin to be replaced by self-assurance.

Kyle works Thumblina in an elongated stay.

Teaching your child to work with your pet will also be helpful in establishing the proper social hierarchy. A dog should never place itself over any family member.

Puppy Social Behavior

Dogs go through many physical and social stages. The best training time is from two to four months of age, because their minds are like sponges soaking up all their experiences, making them both impressionable and responsive. Everything they learn at this age will remain with them throughout their lives.

Several things are happening during this formative time. First, they are acclimating to their new family pack. Second, their baby teeth are being replaced by their permanent teeth. This is a very "oral" time, just as it would be for a two-year-old human. Everything goes in the mouth to discover whether it might be edible or fun to play with.

The first year of a pup's social development can be likened to that of a human from age one to 21. A young puppy (two to four months) is socially similar to a child aged four to seven years. While the attention span may be short, the amount of information learned is at its highest point. The more fun a youngster has while learning, the less resistant he will be to new input as he gets older. Parents also tend to be more tolerant of mistakes, allowing disruption and incorrect responses to some extent, in order to encourage the correct responses.

This is the best time to begin training. Although the pup's attention span and tolerance of work will be short, you will make more progress. Keeping the training sessions short and fun will yield the best response.

In dog packs, domestic or wild, older dogs tolerate a variety of indiscretions on the part of the younger pack members. They understand the puppies have no knowledge of the social order. Through socialization with other pack members, puppies learn which dogs are dominant or submissive. A pup will begin as a subordinate but is driven, through instinct, to work his way up the hierarchical ladder, testing other pack members. As he reaches adolescence, the other canines will begin putting him in his place with quick, decisive reprimands. As the dog gets older, the reprimands will become increasingly firmer.

Just as the puppy learns social behaviors from his dog pack, he must also learn the proper behavior in his new family pack. He will look to you for guidance, seeing you as leader. If you are consistent, reinforcing all proper behaviors and correcting the bad ones, your puppy will be happy to comply. He won't know any other way.

A puppy from five to six months of age is similar to a preadolescent child. He begins to experience hormonal changes, as well as having enormous teething pain with his back teeth coming in. This is when the worst chewing begins. There is also a marked increase in activity, although the attention span remains short.

When your puppy reaches six to seven months of age, he has entered his most difficult developmental period. The hormones are in full swing, making the dog do things that he *knows* are incorrect. Most of the dog's dominance testing occurs at this time, occasionally making the animal difficult to live with. His energy level is very high, causing lots of mischievous behavior—much the same as you might expect from a human teenager.

Kyle gives Thumblina the down command.

At eight to ten months, your dog will still be testing your authority. However, if you have maintained your dominant position and consistency up to this point, you will see a slow decrease in the difficult behavior. Remain watchful, however, for devious behavior that occurs behind your back.

By the time your pet reaches ten months the teething is over, he understands his environment, and will behave properly most of the time. You can expect to experience a few bad days now and then.

Throughout this developmental period there are several ages in particular that you should be aware of. The ages four months and nine months present certain behaviors that can ultimately lead to difficulties later on. These are fear imprint periods. During this time, any bad experiences are imprinted on the canine's brain, causing a phobic reaction throughout its life. It is, therefore, particularly important to make sure all experiences are positive and enjoyable, especially the training.

Canine Perception

Levels of perception vary greatly from one dog breed to another. You must, therefore, make a point to read more about your breed to understand your pet's abilities—his characteristics, personality traits, and strengths and weaknesses. Dogs utilize every sense to interpret their environment. The most used are those of sight, sound, and smell.

While dogs don't have great eyesight, they do perceive movement accurately. They also can see well in twilight, and can perceive some colors, such as green and yellow. They cannot recognize an unmoving object in the distance or a solid see-through barrier directly in front of them. Thus, there are the occasions of dogs going through screens or windows.

Dogs do not have stereoscopic vision because their eyes are set more toward the sides of their head, but they do have very good peripheral vision. Therefore, do not worry if you give a command and your dog isn't looking directly at you. You can be sure he saw it in the periphery.

Dogs mostly communicate using body language. A twist of the ears, movement of the tail, or curvature of the body conveys messages to other canines.

Sound is a secondary form of communication. It is most prominent in the messages between a mother and her pups. Dogs have both a higher and lower frequency range than humans, allowing them to hear about twenty times better than we can. So, if your dog doesn't respond to a command it is not because he did not hear you, but rather because he chose not to respond.

Dogs can cue in on a source of sound by rotating their ears and cocking their heads. Therefore, if your dog is paying attention to you his ears should be set sideways and low. If his ears are perked forward, he is alert to some other sound rather than paying attention to you.

Canines not only receive messages from you through their use of sight and sound, but also through scent. Chemical messages, called pheromones, are emitted through the sweat from a dog's foot pads, as well as his saliva and anal glands. When your dog receives a chemical message from you, it will most likely be through your sweat glands. Everybody excretes sebum, a fatty lubricant substance containing pheromones, from every pore of their body. With the canine's ability to smell as much as a million times better than a human, it knows your mood sometimes before you realize you are experiencing it. You may, at times, think your dog is reading your mind. This is simply a learned response through many hours of interaction, where he has learned what actions accompany your scent.

Because your dog is accustomed to reading your body language and determining your mental and physical state through scent, you should be sure you are in the proper frame of mind to help bring about a successful training session. If you are in an angry mood, your dog will also become testy and upset. If you are distracted in any way, do not expect your pet to maintain his attention, either. Remaining positive and enthusiastic during every training session will increase the enjoyment and satisfaction both for you and your dog.

The sense of taste is another means of acquiring your dog's attentiveness during training. Dogs do have taste buds, some more sensitive than others. Food has a very strong pull on a dog. He will remember *every* behavior or situation in which he has received food. This can be a training aid when working with young puppies, aged two to four months, or for overly submissive or frightened dogs. It gives them a greater incentive to perform, expanding both attentiveness and tolerance levels. A food reward can also be an aid in obtaining perfection. If your dog heels with you but is sloppy, the food can give him incentive to clean up his movements, making them crisper and more exact.

I do not recommend, however, relying on food to train your dog, for this can make him unreliable in distraction situations. Most dogs can be gradually phased out of the use of food rewards, so begin to do so as soon as your dog is working properly with enthusiasm.

3. Dog and Puppy Care

THE CARE YOU GIVE your dog as a new member of your family will affect his behavior later in his life. It is essential that you understand how to treat him.

First, you must make sure to teach any children in your household responsible ways of handling and playing with the new puppy. Very few puppies will tolerate ear and tail pulling, or excessively rough play. The puppy does not understand this torment, and may lash out with a bite, particularly if its warnings, or growls, are ignored. This behavior can lead to aggressive biting later in his life, and he may learn to bite at the children simply because he is not getting his own way.

You should forestall any aggressive behavior from the very beginning by observing a few simple rules:

- Never let the children play with the puppy's mouth.

- Never allow the children to torment the puppy.

- Always observe them while they are together.

- Teach the children to play gently and politely.

- Remember that your puppy will also need his space and time to himself.

While playing with a puppy, it is best to sit on the floor or ground. This will discourage him from jumping on you or your furniture to get your attention. Sitting on the floor with the puppy also designates the times the puppy is allowed to run around and be rambunctious.

When puppies play, they grab each other by the legs and wrestle. If the puppy causes pain to its playmate, the playmate "yips." This yipping is a signal to the aggressor that the bite is painful, and the aggressor responds by letting up or playfully attacking a different area. In order for your puppy to have the most fun playing with you, grab gently at his legs, pull softly, and tumble around with him. If the puppy gets out of hand, biting or barking excessively, you should immediately stop the game. In so doing, you are teaching the puppy he must regulate his aggressive tendencies during playtime.

Just as important as discouraging biting is reminding family members not to overcoddle. Not only will the puppy want to be held and coddled later in life—which can prove difficult with any breed reaching over ten pounds—but he will tend to become insecure by himself, causing many emotionally driven behavior problems as he grows.

For example, everyone might coddle a new puppy for the first couple of weeks and then begin ignoring it because the newness has worn off. From the puppy's viewpoint something is wrong. Its people are no longer maintaining the status quo. (Why can't I be picked up whenever I wish, anymore?) To occupy himself he may begin chewing on the first thing he can find. (Did chewing on the table leg get your attention? Okay, I'll do it again since you touched me when I did it last time.) The destruction has begun!

While a puppy needs petting, massaging, and play, it also needs time alone. If you promote this while the puppy is young, you can reduce the chances of having problems leaving it alone as it gets older.

There will be times you will have to hold your puppy. When doing so, follow these guidelines:

- Be sure you support him securely by placing one hand on his chest between his forelegs, and the other arm around his rump, with your hand holding the hind legs.

- Never suffocate by hugging too tightly.

- If your puppy begins to struggle, it means he is uncomfortable. Redress the situation. If you are not holding him properly, it is best to put him down before he becomes aggressive. Try again when he's had a chance to calm down.

Two-year-old Choco, an Australian Shepherd, in a down/stay and Tanner, his five-month-old sibling, sitting.

When your puppy first arrives, there will be a period of adjustment. The puppy will constantly want attention and, for a while, you will make every effort to accommodate him. This comes easily at first, but you will soon realize that other things are suffering because of it. You cannot spend your entire life catering to the puppy.

You Have a Life, Too!

We all have jobs to attend to, whether they entail working at home or away. You will need to address this situation even before your puppy's arrival. What do we do with the cute little canine while we're not able to watch him? Leave him alone in the house? Would you do that with a five-month-old baby? No. Any responsible parent wouldn't leave a child alone in an unprotected area, such as a crib or playpen. Why do so with a puppy? They are children too!

The best place for any new pet is an enclosed area. You should cover the entire area with protective material in case of accidents. The area should be small enough to make him feel secure, but big enough so he can turn around, play, or stretch out.

My recommendation is a bathroom, kitchen, alcove, or mud room. Such a room should remain open—not closed off with doors, but only with baby gates. This way your puppy won't feel so cut off from the rest of the family. In addition, he will begin feeling more territorial in his new home if he has his own special place.

For an older dog—that is, housebroken and not destructive—his place can be a particular rug or bed placed in a corner of the family room or kitchen. Keep in mind that your dog wants to be with you at all times—it is basic pack instinct, which you should promote, especially with a new dog. Also keep in mind that the dog in sight is less destructive than the one out of sight.

Any new pet must be introduced gradually to your home, one room at a time. Begin with the room where you spend most of your time, and that has an easy-to-clean floor. Once your pet learns to behave in this first enclosure, gradually allow him into others. Always bear in mind that you must watch him constantly in order to correct him as he does something inappropriate.

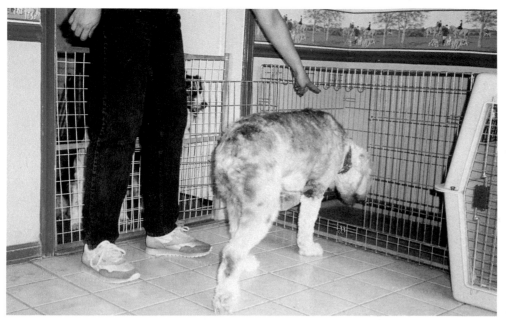

Teaching your dog to kennel-up. The door is open and you throw a treat inside, as you point and give the command.

that the appropriate crate is actually one size larger than manufacturers' suggestions, to ensure that your dog has space to stand at full height without having to keep his head down.

When you have the crate set at the proper size, there will be enough room for the dog, but not enough room for him to mess on one side and lie on the other. If you allow this, you will cause house-training problems difficult to correct. The space may be tight, but remember your puppy will feel more secure, and will tend to control himself better.

Crate Training

Crate-training your puppy is an excellent method of teaching him where his place is. It provides a den-like atmosphere in which your pet will feel very secure as well as be kept out of trouble. Whenever you can't watch him for more than thirty seconds, place him in his crate. Your relationship will be the better for it.

Proper training is very important in getting your pet to accept the concept of the crate. You cannot just stick him in the crate and expect him to be happy. He won't understand and may cry or howl, both of which vocalizations would have elicited responses from his mother while he was living with his litter mates.

Begin the crate training by obtaining one that is the appropriate size for your dog. He should have enough space to stand, turn around, lie down, or chew a toy. If you cannot obtain different sizes of crate to accommodate your growing dog, then just buy one that will fit him at full size, and obtain a divider that you can adjust as he grows. I have found

In training your pet to accept the crates do the following:

- Put a comfortable blanket or bed of some sort if you have a puppy. Many new puppies will feel more comfortable if you place a few stuffed animals in with them.

- Coax your dog into the crate with treats. Praise your dog in a gentle and enthusiastic tone of voice as your dog enters the crate to eat the treat.

- As your dog walks in and out of the crate, be sure not to close the door. Your dog needs to feel comfortable with his new "den" before you begin to confine him in it.

- After a few sessions with your dog going into the crate for a treat, begin to use a word to associate with the crate, such as *kennel*. As you say this word, throw the treat into the crate. When your dog enters, praise him.

Once your dog is inside, you close the door for a few seconds as you continue praising him. As your dog becomes accustomed to the crate, shut the door for increasingly longer periods.

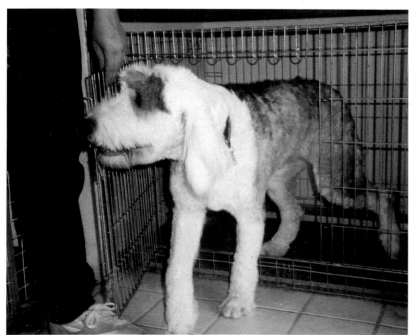

Release your dog from the crate by opening the door and saying "Break" or "Free Dog."

- After your dog has done this several times, begin to close the door briefly. Be sure to praise and give your dog more treats as he remains in the crate.

- After about thirty seconds, let him out.

- Continue in this manner, increasing the time he remains in there each time you say "Kennel" and throw in the treat.

- Once your dog begins to relax inside the crate, lying down or chewing a toy, it is time to leave the room briefly. Begin by leaving for two to five minutes. When you return, open the crate and pet your dog as he remains inside; then let him out.

- The next time you leave the room, do so for ten minutes. Continue in this manner until you have accomplished leaving your dog alone in the crate for an hour, with you in another room. Whenever you return to your dog, praise him calmly and open the crate. You can also give him a treat if you wish.

- Once you have accomplished the hour-long confinement, you can begin to leave the house while your dog is enclosed in the crate. Please take note, however, that you should never leave your dog in a crate over four to five hours without somebody letting him out. If you tend to be away from home more than this amount of time, you should find a neighbor, friend, or dog-walking service to let your pet stretch his legs and relieve himself during midday.

After a few days of these procedures your new dog should not feel at all threatened about being closed in the crate. In fact, he will come to associate it positively and go in willingly.

If your dog is to be outside, there are also rules you must follow. First, never tie your dog to a tree, fence, or any other object. This practice will result in a vicious, uncontrollable dog. Your dog will not receive the proper amount of attention if it is confined in such a manner; it is very easy to forget a pet that is restrained. Each time you start to pet him, he may jump on you. If you intend to tie your dog outside, you must consider getting another type of pet. A dog is a social animal and must be treated as such. Would you tie your children outside just to avoid cleaning up after them? If you insist on keeping your dog outside, you must strive to be humane. Build a fence that will allow him room to exercise. You must also remember that your dog needs attention and play to be properly socialized and incorporated into your family.

Another consideration in tying your dog is the damage he will do to the grass in that area. A dog runs in a pattern and, when left alone for long periods, will begin digging. Digging is a very difficult behavior to correct. You will soon see a "lunar landscape" around the area where you have tied your dog.

Some dogs that are tied for long periods tend to pull on their tethers. This can cause severe damage to their throat. I have seen the results of a dog tied up with a choke chain; the chain became embedded in the animal's throat. It had a scar halfway around its neck. If you insist on tying your dog, exercise some caution, and use either a harness or a comfortable collar—never a choke chain.

The best place for any puppy or dog is with you. While you are at home, the animal should be with you at all times. This promotes a feeling of security for the dog, and allows you to keep an eye on him to prevent any undesirable behavior.

Cherry, a happy thirteen-year-old Springer Spaniel, lying in her bed that is strategically placed in the family room. This allows her to remain with the family in her own private space.

This little bit of preventive medicine will make for a happier dog and a more trusting owner. Your dog is looking to you for guidance. Without that guidance, he can become a pest. It is only fair to yourself and your pet to teach him the limitations and boundaries of your home. Would you do any less for your child, or roommate?

Grooming

Grooming is a very important aspect of caring for your pet, routinely done at least every two or three days. Depending on the breed of dog I recommend a weekly bath, especially for house pets.

Consistent routines will help you to easily recognize any abnormalities in your dog's physique, keeping flea and tick infestation under control as well as allowing you to recognize when your dog is injured or sick. Abnormalities such as lesions, dry skin, or unusual odors can be recognized quickly through these routine examinations. This early detection can save you hundreds of dollars in veterinary bills, and may even save your dog's life.

Every breed requires different types of clips and other special handling. For example, dogs with floppy ears require frequent ear cleanings and special attention when bathing to avoid the development of ear infections. Any dog with skin folds, such as a bulldog, needs to have these folds cleaned regularly or fungus can develop.

It is a good idea to get your puppy used to routine bathing during his first week in your home. Be careful to use only special baby or puppy shampoo, for just like a human infant he is sensitive to strong detergents.

This first bath will set the standard for how he will behave in future baths; so to make sure it is a positive experience, do the following:

- Place your puppy in the empty tub, or deep sink, with a nonslip mat underneath him. Speak calmly, caress him, and give him a treat or two.

- Take your puppy out of the tub, or deep sink while you fill it with warm water.

- When you have filled the tub to about four inches (10cm), place your puppy in it—gently.

- Fill a cup with some of the warm water and let the water spill across his legs.

Teeth cleaning should be done weekly. This ensures healthy gums, and helps in determining early dental problems. Grab the dog's upper lip over the top of his muzzle. Pull up the lips so that you can easily reach his teeth with the toothbrush. Brush gently in a circular motion, allowing your dog occasionally to relax and lick the meat-flavored toothpaste. Praise your dog throughout the experience.

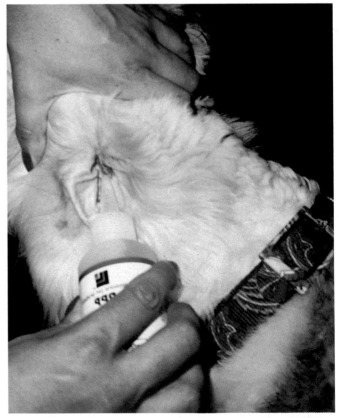

To apply ear cleaner, grab a firm hold of your dog's head, holding his ear back. Squirt the ear cleaner into his ear, rub the ear gently, and then, using a cotton ball, clean out the dirt.

- When he accepts this, begin working your way up his body with the water. First wet his legs, then sides, then rear, then neck, and finally the head, using a sponge.

- Once your puppy is fully wet, work in the shampoo.

- To rinse, do so in the same fashion as your initial soaking.

- After your puppy is rinsed, drain the tub and wrap him in a towel as you rub him dry.

The entire process should be done with much praise and coaxing. It also makes the event more pleasant if you give your puppy a few treats throughout.

If you have obtained your dog as an adult and wish to bathe him, either use a garden hose, if it is above 70 degrees F (21 degrees C) outside, or do the following in order to make sure the experience is not a negative one:

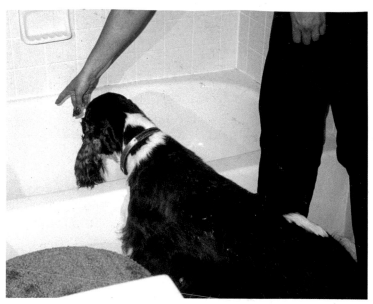

Teaching your dog to get into the bathtub. Begin with the same procedure as crate training. The tub should be dry. Throw the treat into the tub and say, "Inside!"

Once he is in the tub, tell your dog to assume sit/stays and down/stays. All of these positions are required for a thorough bath.

- Get your dog used to the tub by taking him into it when it is dry. Either coax or bait him in. Make it a fun game by throwing in a treat or toy for him to retrieve.

- Once your dog is not afraid of going into the tub, fill it with water to about four inches (10cm). Coax your dog in by using the same devices used previously.

- When your dog enters the tub, give him a lot of praise.

- Begin bathing him by taking cupfuls of the water in the tub and pouring it over his legs. While you do this, talk soothingly and praise your pet enthusiastically.

- As your dog begins to relax, move the water in cupfuls up his legs and over his back.

- When your dog is fully soaked, begin working in the soap by starting at his neck and chest. Gradually work your way across his back and down his legs. Once he is fully soaped, begin to rinse in the same manner you began his first soaking with the water.

The down/stay is useful for initial soaking as well as for rinsing.

The stand/stay is useful for soaping.

- When your pet is rinsed, drain the water from the tub, and rub him briskly with a thick towel.

- Once done let your pet come out of the tub on his own, as you continue praising him. Be sure to keep him indoors until he is completely dry to prevent him from catching a chill or from rolling in the dirt and ruining all your hard work.

- Drain the tub, prepare for a shake, and then towel-dry as he remains in a stand/stay. Be sure to towel off his feet or you will have wet footprints everywhere.

If you are bathing an obedience-trained dog, then the bathing process can be much easier.

- Fill the tub with water up to eight inches (20cm) or more.

- Coax your dog into the tub with toys or food. Once your dog learns that going into the tub can be rewarding, he will learn to go in on command.

- Place your dog in a down/stay as you soak him with water.

- Then put your pet into a stand/stay as you soap him.

- Once he is thoroughly soaped, put him into a down/stay again to rinse him off.

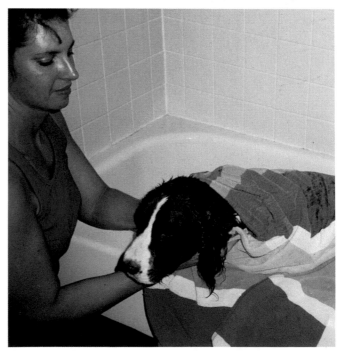

The stand/stay is also useful for towel-drying.

Regular Examinations

Physical examinations of your dog should be systematic. Begin at the head and work your way carefully to the rear, massaging with your fingers to feel the dog's skin. This will help you detect any abnormal lumps or abrasions. This is especially important when checking for ticks. Ticks tend to gather under the legs, between the toes, around the ears and eyes, and on the neck.

Examining a dog from the animal shelter. The dog is happy to allow a checkup provided the hands touching him are gentle and soothing. It helps to speak to the dog in a quiet, calm manner. In this way even the most skittish dog will allow an examination.

It is also important to have your dog clipped routinely. Not only does this improve the appearance of your dog, but it also helps rid him of mats that can become cluttered with burrs and other debris. Consulting a book on your dog's breed will give you the advice you need to meet the pet's grooming requirements. If you follow the grooming advice and clip the fur once a month, you can save yourself costly visits to a groomer. Your dog much prefers that *you* attend to his grooming needs. If you had the choice of a good grooming effort from your master, or being taken to some strange place where you are left alone in a cage and handled by an unfamiliar person, what would you choose?

I have also found that several food additives can be put into your dog's regular diet to help maintain a healthy coat and skin. A combination of brewer's yeast and garlic can help provide a glossy coat as well as cut down on flea infestations. Linatone or a little oil (teaspoon) daily helps keep the coat and skin moist. Another helpful supplement is a soft-boiled egg once a week.

Before adding any of these ingredients you may wish to try them in small quantities to ensure they do not bother your dog. If you find a loose stool, then discontinue their use, and consult with your veterinarian regarding a safer supplement.

Grooming Requirements

Below is a listing of seventy-two of the most popular breeds and their grooming requirements. Each dog will fall under one of the three categories:

Minimal—brush and check every two or three days
Moderate—brush and check every other day
Daily—brush and check every day

This listing is not absolute, and assumes that the dog receives a regular clipping (every six to eight weeks). The grooming requirements vary according to your pet's clip and exercise level, and where he chooses to run. A dog running through woods, in a swamp, or at the beach will require more frequent bathing and examinations.

Popular Breeds and Their Grooming Requirements

Minimal—brush and check every two or three days **Moderate**—brush and check every other day **Daily**—brush and check every day

Breed	Minimal	Moderate	Daily	Breed	Minimal	Moderate	Daily
Afghan Hound			•	Doberman Pinscher	•		
Airedale Terrier		•		English Setter		•	
Akita		•		English Springer Spaniel		•	
Alaskan Malamute		•		English Toy Spaniel		•	
American Staffordshire	•			German Shepherd		•	
Australian Shepherd		•		German Shorthair Pointer	•		
Basset Hound	•			Golden Retriever		•	
Beagle	•			Gordon Setter		•	
Bearded Collie			•	Great Dane	•		
Belgian Sheepdog			•	Great Pyreneees			•
Belgian Tervuren		•		Irish Setter		•	
Bernese Mountain Dog			•	Irish Wolfhound		•	
Bichon Frise			•	Keeshond			•
Bloodhound	•			Kerry Blue Terrier		•	
Border Collie		•		Labrador Retriever	•		
Border Terrier	•			Lhasa Apso			•
Borzoi		•		Maltese			•
Boston Terrier	•			Newfoundland			•
Bouvier des Flandres		•		Norfolk Terrier	•		
Boxer	•			Norwegian Elkhound		•	
Briard			•	Old English Sheepdog			•
Brittany Spaniel		•		Poodle		•	
Bull Terrier	•			Pug	•		
Bulldog	•			Rhodesian Ridgeback	•		
Bullmastiff		•		Rottweiler	•		
Cairn Terrier		•		Saint Bernard			•
Catahoula Leopard	•			Samoyed			•
Chesapeake Bay Retriever	•			Schipperke	•		
Long-coated Chihuahua		•		Schnauzer	•		
Smooth-coated Chihuahua	•			Scottish Terrier		•	
Chow Chow		•		Shetland Sheepdog			•
Cocker Spaniel		•		Shih Tzu			•
Rough-coated Collie			•	Siberian Husky		•	
Smooth-coated Collie		•		Weimaraner	•		
Corgi		•		Welsh Terrier	•		
Longhair Dachshund		•		West Highland White Terrier		•	
Shorthair Dachshund	•			Whippet	•		
Dalmatian	•			Yorkshire Terrier		•	

Lady, a Rottweiler, is sitting in the proper place while in a vehicle: the backseat.

Exercise

Recreation is mandatory for a dog's good physical and mental health. Any dog, no matter what size, enjoys a good run. If you live in the city, take your dog to a park or drive to the country and stop at a farm. Dogs love the smells and excitement of a farm. This change of scenery is very helpful to the dog's mental attitude. A dog enjoys going for a ride in the car with his master, and will always look forward to a good time whenever you take him along. This is helpful in teaching your dog to become accustomed to the car.

There will always come a time when you cannot avoid a car ride, such as a trip to the veterinarian. This early training will enable you to drive safely with your dog and prevent damage to the car's interior during the ride. Before taking your dog in the car for the first time, make sure he has an empty stomach. This may help prevent your dog from vomiting and spoiling your upholstery. Many dogs need to take several rides to help overcome motion sickness. Be sure to be prepared with lots of paper towels and a trash bag. You may even want to put newspaper on the seats to aid in cleaning the mess.

If your dog is very active in the car, it is a good idea to obtain a wire-mesh kennel and place the dog inside during its initial experiences. This will help you avoid any accidents caused by your dog jumping on you while you are driving. Once your dog has learned some basic obedience, you can teach him to remain in the backseat without hanging over you or out the window. It is not a good idea to begin traveling with your puppy by putting him in your lap as you drive. Not only can this cause serious problems when you try to train him to remain in the back, but it can also take your mind off your driving.

If you begin the right way, there won't be any trauma for either you or the puppy.

Exercise Requirements

The following chart includes seventy-two of the most popular breeds, summarizing each breed's exercise requirements:

> **Minimal**—okay in small yard, doesn't require long walks
>
> **Moderate**—needs large yard and several walks per day (more while young)
>
> **Maximum**—needs large yard, several walks per day, as well as free-roaming time to run

Not every dog adheres to its own breed characteristics. Not only are there individual differences but there are also age and environmental differences. A dog will vary greatly in its exercise requirements between puppyhood and adulthood. Puppies generally have more energy, therefore require more exercise in short, frequent increments. An adult dog will do better with longer, but not as frequent, exercise.

An elderly dog will not want to go out as often as a younger dog and will not want to run around as much. He tends to go outside only to relieve himself and then wants to return to his warm bed.

Environmental factors such as the weather can change a dog's exercise requirements accordingly. If the weather is very hot the dog will not want to exercise for a long period, especially if it is a large, long-haired breed. When the weather is cool, most dogs feel very feisty and require more exercise. If it is windy outside, then dogs will be very distracted and may not listen as well as they normally would. Rain

Popular Breeds and Their Exercising Requirements

Minimal Exercise Requirement—okay in small yard, doesn't require long walks

Basset Hound	Dachshund	Pug
Bulldog	English Toy Spaniel	Scottish Terrier
Bullmastiff	Maltese	Shih Tzu
Chihuahua	Mastiff	West Highland White Terrier
Corgi	Norfolk Terrier	Yorkshire Terrier

Moderate Exercise Requirement—needs large yard, and several walks per day (more while young)

Afghan Hound	Chow Chow	Norwegian Elkhound
Airedale Terrier	Cocker Spaniel	Old English Sheepdog
Akita	Collie	Rottweiler
Bernese Mountain Dog	English Springer Spaniel	Saint Bernard
Bichon Frise	German Shepherd	Schnauzer
Bloodhound	Great Pyrenees	Shetland Sheepdog
Borzoi	Irish Wolfhound	Toy and Miniature Poodle
Boston Terrier	Keeshond	Weimaraner
Bouvier des Flandres	Kerry Blue Terrier	Whippet
Briard	Lhasa Apso	
Cairn Terrier	Newfoundland	

Maximum Exercise Requirement—needs large yard, several walks per day, as well as free-roaming time to run

Alaskan Malamute	Boxer	Gordon Setter
American Staffordshire	Brittany Spaniel	Irish Setter
Australian Shepherd	Bull Terrier	Labrador Retriever
Beagle	Catahoula Leopard	Rhodesian Ridgeback
Bearded Collie	Chesapeake Bay Retriever	Samoyed
Belgian Sheepdog	Dalmatian	Schipperke
Belgian Tervuren	Doberman Pinscher	Siberian Husky
Border Collie	German Shorthair Pointer	Welsh Terrier
Border Terrier	Golden Retriever	

can also affect some breeds of dogs. I have seen that many of the short-coated breeds do not like to sit in a wet area and may either completely refuse the sit command or crouch on their hindquarters. Many "spoiled" dogs will act in this manner also. By saying they are spoiled, I mean their *owners* will not walk them in the rain.

The companionship you give your dog is invaluable. The more attention and time you spend with him, the more devoted to you he will become. This is also excellent therapy for you. It gives you a time to release yourself from the frustrations of your day and just enjoy the companionship and fun your dog can provide. The more time you spend with your dog, the closer your bonds become, and the better you can communicate with each other.

Some dogs like to play special games, such as fetch or roughhousing. Try to take some time out of your busy schedule to play these games. You will find it both enjoyable and relaxing.

In Chapter 18, I will describe several games that are not only enjoyable, but increase your dog's awareness and intelligence level.

Dogs need their own toys. If a dog does not have his own designated toys, he will look to your shoes, furniture, or other household items as substitutes. Rawhide bones, soup bones, and old tennis balls make excellent toys. While some dogs love to play with an old rag tied into knots, so that they can dig their teeth into it and shake it around, I do not recommend this type of toy. Sometimes strings can become lodged in your dog's throat or intestine, causing severe damage.

A Nylabone or Gumabone can replace some of the other chew toys that are not appropriate. These plastic bones can be indestructible by all but the largest breeds, as well as give them many hours of chewing pleasure. Other safe toys include Choo Hooves, solid rubber balls and bones, sterilized cow shank bones, and American-made rawhide. You will know American-made rawhide by the bleached white color. I do not recommend, however, that you give your dog any chips or sticks, for they may become lodged in his throat.

To keep your dog interested in his toys, rotate them. Give your dog three toys one day, and replace them with three different toys the next day. This retains his interest.

Never let your dog make one of your treasured household items into his own toy. If you allow that to happen even once, you may never find peace again. Your dog will simply take whatever he wishes to play with without your permission. If this occurs, consult a professional dog trainer for in-home counseling. A good trainer can explain how to correct this behavior problem. Keep in mind that every dog is different and may respond well to some methods while not to others.

4. Training Equipment

❖

BEFORE OBTAINING TRAINING equipment you will need to consider your individual needs. If you are working with a puppy under three months old, you should use a flat buckle or snap-on collar. This way you will not damage the youngster's trachea. By the time he reaches three months or older he will require a regular training collar. There are several types I recommend, again depending on the age and size of the dog.

For a small breed of dog or a young dog that doesn't pull on the leash, a large-link choke chain, lightweight with rounded links, will be best. The Barbara Woodhouse training collar can be utilized for the purpose of noise only.

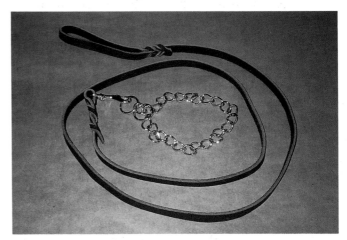

The choke chain and six-foot leather leash.

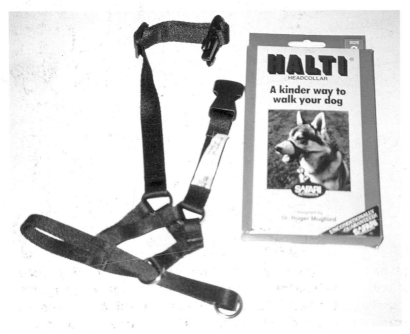

Halti head collar.

For those of you who have a dog that already pulls on the lead, or is very large, I suggest using a Halti head collar. This will guide your pet's head, without choking or hurting him. It will also allow you to use leverage rather than muscle when guiding him into different training positions.

The leash you use should be a six-foot leather or cotton-web leash. If your dog is of the larger variety, I suggest the leather leash in order to prevent rope burns. A smaller breed of dog can work well with a cotton-web leash. The lead should be a half-inch wide for optimum grip.

When acquiring these items, there are several rules to consider. First of all, if you are using a choke chain, measure your dog to determine the proper length. Measure the dog's head from the top of his skull and around under his jaw. Add two inches to this measurement and you will have the size for the chain you should buy. The Barbara Woodhouse choke chains tend to run a bit small. If you are going to be using the recommended choke chain, you should add four inches to the dog's measurement, rather than two. If your dog's measurement is an odd number, go up one size. Choke chains come in even sizes. For example, if your dog's head measures 13 inches, buy a 16-inch chain. The measurement of the choke chain is very important for proper and expedient training.

You must be sure to put your dog's choke chain on properly. Run the chain through one of the rings at the end. As you face the dog, the "running" part of the collar, or the part that moves as you jerk, should be coming out of the ring on your left side.

The proper application of the choke chain.

Measure your dog's head by placing measuring tape from the top, down under his jaw, and back up to the top. Add two inches to the measurement and round off to the next-highest even number. This will ensure a properly fitted choke chain.

Properly applied choke chain. The two rings meet behind the dog's right ear, with the chain slipping over the back of the neck. This ensures that the chain will automatically release when it has been applied during training.

A good rule of thumb is that as you slip the chain over your dog's head, it should resemble the letter P. If you put the chain on incorrectly, it will not release after a jerk, but will remain tight around your dog's neck, constricting the dog's throat. This will make the entire training session very unpleasant for your dog, and will not accomplish the desired results.

An improperly applied choke chain. The slip is coming from underneath the neck, which will cause the chain to catch, pulling tighter when you use it.

If you are using a Halti, read the back of the box and follow the directions for sizing. Your dog should have plenty of room in the muzzle area, but the Halti should be very snug around his head, behind his ears. If it is not snug, your dog will easily be able to remove it.

You will need the six-foot leather leash for several reasons. First, throughout the time you work with the dog on the leash, the leash must remain loose. It should be hanging down to your dog's right shoulder, when using a choke chain, and down to his neck, if using a Halti. This allows enough slack in the lead to properly correct your dog should he lunge or pull. A short lead would not allow for the proper correction. Also, you will have a tendency to pull a lot when you are holding your dog tightly. The more you pull on your dog the more he will pull back. The leather leash offers you a firmer grip, not burning your hand if it slides through. The leather leash may cost a bit more but will last a long time, softening with age.

Make sure you attach the leash to the "running" part of the collar, to ensure that when you snap, the collar will contract and release quickly.

When you are face-to-face with your dog, the chain should look like a P.

The six-foot leash attaches to the slip part of the chain that goes over the neck.

If you attach the leash to the incorrect ring of the Halti you will be tugging ineffectively, as well as choking your dog. The other items you'll need are a 15- to 20-foot cotton-web line. You will use this in your advanced obedience training. Do not use this lead until you are absolutely sure of your dog on the six-foot lead in all phases of obedience. This lead will give you control over your pet from a greater distance. Your dog will learn you can control him from anywhere. I will expand upon the uses of this lead and those of the three-foot cotton rope when we begin advanced training.

Another item you'll need in advanced training is a short pull tab. A clothesline rope works nicely. You can buy this in any grocery store, and get 50 feet at one time. Cut off one and a half feet (for a small dog) or three feet (for a big dog).

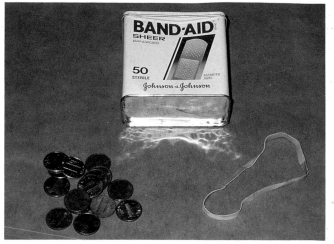

The "no-jump" box. A metal box with fifteen pennies. The elastic keeps the box closed while it is shaken.

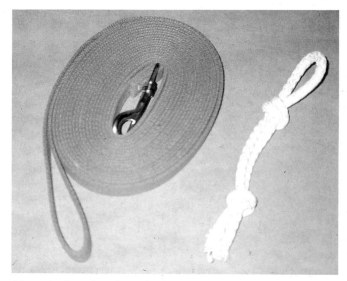

Twenty-foot leash and cotton pull tab.

Fold it in half, then tie a knot closing the two loose ends, and tie another knot in the middle. Attach the tab to the collar with a half-hitch knot.

A throw chain or can with pennies in it will also be helpful in behavior problem correction. The throw chain needs to make a sharp sound. If you choose to use the "no-jump" box, you can easily make one with a metal Band-Aid box, coffee can, or tea tin. Then simply add about fifteen pennies to it, secure it with an elastic, and you have a very useful tool.

Things to Remember before Training Your Dog

As a general rule never give a command that you are unable to back up. For example, if you tell your dog to sit and he does not comply, you must be ready to place him in the sit immediately. If you do not back up your commands, your dog will learn to ignore you, or to associate the words with another behavior.

When I communicate with a dog, I use tones that are natural to his canine language. This facilitates a quick response from the dog and complete understanding within a very short time. There are three distinct tones of voice. If these tones are used on an everyday basis and consistently, then your dog will begin to learn the words associated with the tones, thus forming a "vocabulary."

Praise tone—This is a high, enthusiastic tone. You might think of the praise tone as almost a "baby talk" sound but not quite so high in frequency. If you praise too enthusiastically you will break your dog's attention. Through trial and error you will learn the correct frequency to use.

It is very important to let your pet know when he is responding properly. This will encourage good behavior. The more enthusiastic you are with your praise, the more animated your dog will be. I have trained dogs that have been so happy working that their toes nearly touch their noses with their enthusiastic prancing. I enjoy working with a dog that is having fun, and the dog enjoys working for a person who is also having a good time. Your dog will know immediately if you are genuinely happy with his actions.

Your praise should be constant the entire time your dog is behaving correctly. This keeps his mind on you instead of on his surroundings; it promotes attentiveness. There are some dogs, however, that react poorly to constant chatter. These dogs will forge ahead every time they hear the praise. You can overcome this behavior by doing a turn every time they forge ahead. I will discuss this further in Chapter 7, which discusses heeling.

In most cases it is wise not to touch your dog while you are praising him. It may disrupt his concentration. There are some dogs, however, that benefit from a light touch during a stay exercise. In order to find out if your dog is one of these you will have to experiment. Every dog is different and may require a different approach to each training behavior.

To teach your dog a word associated with this praise tone, be consistent with the use of one word. I use the word *good*. Such as "Good Boy," "Good Dog," "Good Fido." If you keep all words very simple it will make it easier for your dog to pick up their meanings.

Command tone—This is a tone that is full of authority. Use it when telling your dog to do something, such as sit, down, heel, or stay. You should not draw

Submissive position. You kneel at the dog's level. Use this position for greeting, playing, or releasing the dog from work.

out or repeat the tone. If you wish that your dog would listen on one command, then give only one command.

Before every command you should say your dog's name. Don't say his name harshly, but rather use a pleasant "Hey, you!" tone of voice. Your dog's name should always have pleasant associations. This not only teaches your pet his name, but also gets his attention on you as you give the command. This will avoid needless tugs on the collar, thus keeping the commands positive. You should never jerk your dog's collar when giving a command. Associate all leash jerks with your reprimand tone.

Reprimand tone—This tone is used whenever your dog is incorrect. It is a low, growl tone, very similar to a dog's warning growl. The reprimand should be paired with the word *no*. Any time your dog is misbehaving he should receive your "No!" If you are working him on the leash and he pulls, then you pair the "No!" with a leash jerk. Or, if your dog is in the house and begins sniffing at the garbage, then he gets a "No!" and a push in the direction away from the garbage can.

Your dog must also be aware of when he is or is not under a command. To communicate this to him be sure to release him with a consistent word such as *break*. This is a good word because we don't use it much in our everyday speech. Release words such as *okay* or *that's it!* occur quite often in our ordinary discourse, and so you can find yourself inadvertently releasing your dog when you did not mean to. When you give your dog the release word be sure to use body language that also signifies his release. Crouch down and praise him as you pet him in his favorite areas (chest, stomach, or behind his ears).

You will find that this word is one of the first ones that your dog will learn, for it always has pleasant associations.

Be consistent—You will find that consistency is the key to reliability. If you employ consistent methods in all situations, then your dog will not only learn quickly but will also listen when surrounded by distractions. You must practice consistency in your voice, body language, and visual cues. Use the same tones and words for each exercise. For example, do not use several words for one command. If you tell your dog to heel, do not say "Come on" sometimes and "Heel" other times. Always use the heel command.

To be consistent with your body language keep in mind your two main body positions. Stand or sit upright when giving a command or reprimand, and crouch down when praising or trying to get your dog over intimidation. You can also praise as you stand upright while working with your dog, but you will not get the same response from your command if you are crouched down when giving it.

Your dog will learn to respond to visual commands as he learns from your vocal tones. He will respond more quickly with a consistent signal than with different ones. For example, when telling your dog to heel, always begin on your left leg. Eventually your dog will pick up on this visual signal and will not move when your right leg begins first. If you are inconsistent with which leg you use when giving this command, then your dog will not pick up on the command visually, only vocally. You will find that if you are consistent with both visual and vocal signals your dog will learn faster.

Maintain your training—The training of your dog is an ongoing process. You should not stop training just because you seem to have him doing things properly. You can continue to expand his knowledge and keep him enthusiastic about working, thus keeping him out of trouble.

I have had many phone calls from clients who have told me that their dog has started doing bad things again. My first question to them is "Have you been working with your dog?" Of course their answer is that they have not had the time to do so. I relate to them the importance of maintaining the training with an everyday routine. When they return to this routine, then the bad behaviors disappear. Those horrible things that their dogs were doing were their pets' way of saying "I need attention!"

Maintaining these trained behaviors also means that if your dog "tests" you—and they always do (who has children who don't try to get away with things?)—you must be ready to reinforce his training either with a correction or by placing him in the desired position. If you get casual about reinforcing the training, then your dog will get casual about responding to your commands. Within a short time he will regress and require retraining.

This also means that even though you may be taking your dog for a "fun walk" or out to relieve himself, you do not let him go racing through the door, dragging you down the street. You can maintain simple control by doing a sit/stay at the door, heeling through, closing the door as your dog remains in a sit/stay, and heeling to where you wish to go. Not only is this a lot easier on your arm, but you are also reinforcing your dog's training with everyday routine.

Place your dog in a sit/stay before you walk through any door or gate. This teaches him to never rush through and run off.

Another important point to remember when working with your dog is the matter of distraction. You must be able to concentrate on what you are doing. If you are distracted by your surroundings, then your dog will also be unable to concentrate. Your dog looks to you as a leader. If you want him to follow your directions then you must be sincere when relating them. If you give a command halfway, then your pet will not respond positively. You will need to block out any distractions in order to teach your dog to do the same.

After you have accomplished an exercise it is a good idea to practice the behavior while in a distraction situation. Take your dog to the park or a playground. There are many distractions in these places. Another good distraction is to work on the sidewalk in a shopping center. There are new people and smells everywhere, and your dog must learn to listen despite all of these inviting distractions. It's also a great way to show off your dog. There have been many times when I have taken my clients and their pets into a shopping center and received many comments from passersby about how well the dog behaves. It's great for one's ego.

Training Phases

The very first objective at the onset of training is to achieve attentiveness from your pet. This attentiveness development—**Phase 1**—is the first stage of obedience training. After several minutes of heeling you will see your dog beginning to watch you. This is the first sign that you are developing his attentiveness. Your dog is watching you in order to anticipate your movements, thereby decreasing his chances of receiving a punishment.

Many dogs will begin with their normal pulling routine, only to be checked by you when you turn in the opposite direction (as you will learn when doing the heeling exercises). After several turns you will see your dog slowing down and turning to look at you.

If you are starting with a Halti, your dog will spend the first fifteen minutes trying to get it off his head. Most dogs are not used to wearing things on their faces and may be uncomfortable. Using treats and praise will soon get his attention on you. Do things in small increments. For example, when teaching the heel, move forward just five steps, then stop and reward him.

Some dogs will try to intimidate their trainers by jumping up on them, or biting at the leash. Other dogs may feel intimidated by being told what to do, and being made to follow through. Many intimidated dogs will cry out in frustration, or simply plant themselves and not move. I will explain how to handle these "tricks" that dogs pull later in this chapter, and in Chapter 14, when I address behavior modification.

Another noticeable difference in this first phase is that your dog becomes disciplined in all aspects of his behavior. He will be less rowdy or mischievous. Of course, the more you work him the more tired he will be. A tired dog is less likely to be racing around the house with your sock in his mouth trying to get you to play chase. You do, however, want to limit each session to about fifteen minutes. This is equal to a long romp in the woods.

If you are training an older dog, he may show signs of depression. This is due to his having had the upper hand for a while, and suddenly being put into a "lower" position.

The first phase is very short, lasting several days at the most. **Phase 2** will kick in very quickly, as your pet begins to understand that this is not torture, it is actually a lot of fun—enjoying this interaction and learning experience.

Most dogs look forward to their training sessions. You will notice this when you bring out the training equipment and your pet begins to jump around excitedly. Dogs normally want to please and receive praise from their owners. It is this attribute that has made them "Man's Best Friend."

During Phase 2 your pet will also pick up on the meaning of "No!" If you are firm and consistent in reprimanding your pet for every misbehavior, he will begin to desist and look to you for guidance. This is also developing the "shadow effect." Your dog will begin to follow you everywhere. Be sure to encourage this, for it will keep him out of trouble.

I now have four shadows that follow me from place to place: my three dogs and my cat. They are all part of my family pack and prefer to be where their pack leader is. Of course they can't go everywhere, and this can get annoying if I am going from the family room into the kitchen and back. If I give them the stay command, then I can move about more freely without my shadows, and they are very happy to be listening to their command. Again, this demonstrates how the training can be used in an everyday routine.

Attentive dog.

Your dog will begin looking at you before reacting to a distraction. Be certain to encourage this behavior, for he is only waiting for his pack leader to show how to react to the situation.

During the Phase 2 training process your dog will test you from time to time, but mostly will be very good. Enjoy this while you can, for the next phase is extremely difficult.

Phase 3 usually occurs at the time you are teaching your dog to go down on command. The down is a submissive position, and not many dogs will go down willingly. Phase 3 requires a lot of patience and persistence. Your dog will be constantly testing your leadership capabilities. He may even try to do things he never did before, or has not done in a long time. If you remain firm, then this phase should pass within four to seven days. Do not give in to the smallest infraction or you are in for a longer time in Phase 3.

Phase 4 is much easier than all the previous phases. Your dog has a complete understanding that you are the leader, and he must quickly listen to your command. He will be calmer and rarely get into trouble, will lay down and remain without con-

tention, and understand that it is not such a "bad" thing. At this time you should be nearly finished with your basic obedience training. You will probably be working on the finish and the stand/stay. These commands are very easy for your dog to comprehend, and are even somewhat enjoyable, such as the caressing he receives when in the stand/stay.

Before you begin training a puppy under five months old versus working with an older dog, keep in mind that your puppy will not last much more than ten to fifteen minutes during a training session. An older dog, on the other hand, will have a higher tolerance for the work and may remain attentive for as much as twenty minutes. In both cases he gradually builds up tolerance to the stresses of training. But don't push it. If your pet begins wanting to lie down, looks droopy-eyed, or begins becoming uncontrollable, it is time to stop. Do not, however, stop on a bad note. Always have your dog do something correctly before ending a training session.

While working with your dog you will find that the first few minutes may be difficult while you are trying to obtain your dog's attention. The following ten to fifteen minutes will be the best training time. You will know you are in the prime training time when you see your dog prancing, wagging his tail, and grinning (only a mother knows the difference between a grin and grimace). After this prime training time your pet will tire and not respond as well as at the start. You must begin to think about ending your session. Work your pet a few more minutes in order to build on his tolerance, and then end with something that you know is easy for your dog to perform, such as a sit.

A tired dog will lag and lose interest in work. When you see this behavior, it is time to stop the training session.

Understanding these phases and behaviors will make it easier for you to be successful with these training procedures. Keep them in mind, good luck, and, most of all, have fun!

Tricks That Dogs Pull

Many dogs have a sense of humor. They also learn from experience how to get the upper hand, or in this case "paw." Using this knowledge, they perform "tricks" that can make a training session very difficult. These tricks appear mostly in dogs over the age of five months, for they are learned behaviors. Puppies have not had the time to discover ways of outwitting their owners.

The most common tricks are putting a paw over the lead, jumping on the handler, biting the lead and playing tug, or planting himself on the ground and crying, as if being told what to do is a torturous task.

Before I describe how to cure these "tricks," I will explain how they can come about. First, let's look at the most common of these behaviors: putting a paw over the lead. Many dogs quickly figure out that the source of a handler's control is in the leash attached to the collar around its neck. The dog soon finds

that if he puts his paw over the lead, then it no longer pulls and its handler must stop to unwind it. The reason the dog may form an aversion to the lead is most likely that its handler is pulling incessantly and pointlessly. A trainer should never use a constant pull on a leash to maneuver a dog into any behavior. You should approach all training in such a manner as to ensure that the dog enjoys himself. Rethink your training approach and try to follow the directions as discussed later in Chapter 7. Do not use the lead as a lever; use it as an aid. If your dog puts his foot over the lead while you are heeling, leave the lead where it is until you stop. Put the dog in a sit, then untangle the lead and continue with the exercises. If your dog puts his paw over the lead in a stay—because he knows you will be unable to correct him when he breaks the stay—then immediately untangle the lead and hold it over the dog's head. If your dog gets up, replace him in the stay position and repeat the stay command, continuing to walk around him.

The next dog trick, jumping on the handler, is very common among dogs who have not been taught that jumping up is wrong at any time. To cure the bad habit of jumping, refer to the techniques in Chapter 14 on behavior modification, and then begin to reverse this dog trick.

1. Begin by taking your dog into the heel mode.

2. If he proceeds to jump up, snap the lead in the opposite direction of his "flight pattern," as you say "No" in a low tone of voice. Throughout this correction continue to walk.

If your dog jumps up on you and bites the lead, he is doing so to stop you from pulling on his neck. You should concentrate on snapping rather than pulling when correcting, and do the following:

1. Take your dog into a heel.

2. When he jumps up and grabs the lead, jerk it quickly and firmly from his mouth. If you do this too slowly you will incite your dog into a game of tug-of-war, which he will very much enjoy but is guaranteed to frustrate you.

3. Never stop and try to pull the lead from his mouth; jerk it out as you say "No." If the hard jerk does not work, then place your dog in a sit, tell him to drop, place one hand over the top of his nose, and squeeze his lips into his teeth. As soon as he drops the lead, go back into the heel as you praise him.

The most common of the "dog tricks" is the rear-end "plant." This is when a dog will sit or lie down refusing to move no matter how hard his handler tugs, pulls, or begs. There are also times when a dog will simply test the owner by not moving forward when commanded to do so. The dog remains in the sit, as the handler steps forward. If the handler stops and looks at the dog, then the behavior is immediately set in.

To cure the "planting" trick do the following:

1. Begin the session by standing in the heel position.

2. Give the heel command and step forward on your left leg.

3. DO NOT STOP. No matter what happens, do not stop; give a firm jerk with your "No!" and keep going. If your dog lies down, you may have to give several jerks and half-drag him into the heel. As long as you do not pull, then your dog will not be choked.

4. Every time your dog hesitates, jerk the lead, say "No!" and just keep walking, making certain you do not stop in response to his behavior.

The final "dog trick," that of the crying dog, is probably the most difficult to cure. When a puppy or dog whines, screams, or cries out, our first instinct is to rush to him and comfort him. This humane reaction is the whole reason the dog does this whenever it wants to avoid a situation. Granted, if he is behaving in this manner you should rethink your training approach. You may be going too quickly or using a method that is too harsh for your dog. There are dogs, however, that cry out in frustration. An example is the cry of frustration when a dog has to be returned into a down/stay repeatedly and does not wish to remain there. The dog is not being hurt by being placed into a down; he simply does not wish to comply when there are more fun things to be doing.

The best way to cure the crying dog is to ignore all of his sounds of woe, and persistently make him follow through with whatever you told him to do. If you want him to heel, but he has other ideas, such as sniffing, and crying out, when you insist on his following through with the command, then you will have to steel yourself, use a leash reprimand, and continue on.

If you maintian your level of consistency, you can cure this problem within several training sessions, and you will get a less emotional reaction.

5. Training the Elderly Dog

WHOEVER CAME UP with the saying "You cannot teach an old dog new tricks" simply did not know the correct approach. Every dog is trainable regardless of its age. I have trained dogs from as young as six weeks up to the age of fifteen years. Many of the elderly dogs that I have worked with had chronic behavior problems. Their owners had put up with ten years or more of having a dog make piles in their house every time they would leave or having to put their dog in confinement every time a visitor would come.

I was able to correct these problems with simple basic obedience training.

As with people, the older dogs get, the more set in their behavior patterns they become. Many psychologists say that a child's personality is fully formed by the time it is six years old. If you were to compare this with dogs' years, your dog would be approximately five months old. While it is easier to train a dog when it is at its more receptive age, it is not a lost cause with a dog that is beyond this learning period. You simply must know which "buttons" to push.

Before You Start

Before beginning the training of an older dog you must ask yourself a few questions, the answers to which are the key to successfully solving the behavior problems.

1. When did the behavior begin? Has he always behaved in this manner since puppyhood, or did it begin after a particular event?

2. Did the behavior begin slowly, or did it suddenly appear?

3. What are the stimuli which occur prior to the behavior?

4. How do you try to prevent the behavior from occurring?

Let's try to find the answers to these questions one by one. First, did you put up with this behavior since your dog was a puppy because you were ineffective at correcting the behavior, or because you were inconsistent with your communication?

The answer is to teach your dog basic obedience! You and your dog will learn to communicate. You will learn how to become more consistent so that your dog knows that you really have meaning in your vocal emanations.

Did your dog begin soiling the house after it had been sick, or after it was moved or had some other environmental change? Either of these reasons can cause your dog to slip in his house-training. The answer, again, is to teach your dog basic obedience. Some of you may respond with, "I already went through obedience training." Yes, that may be so, but did you keep up with it? Especially after the change in your pet's environment? If not, go back to work with your dog! He needs his constructive time with you on a daily basis. If you continue with your training, he will maintain his.

I have received occasional calls from former clients who have recently encountered behavior problems with their dogs that were previously very well mannered. These problems ranged from chewing to house soiling. The first question I ask is, "Have you been working with your dog recently?" I normally receive the reply, "No, I have been very busy" with this or that.

In these cases the dog is trying to tell his owners something: "I want attention!" The only way your dog can communicate this to you is to do bad things because they definitely get your attention. The cure is to simply transfer this into a positive mode with the obedience training. Show your dog that he gets more attention when he performs what you ask. Your pet will once again relax and enjoy your company.

Did your pet begin this bad behavior after a traumatic experience? For example, did he begin biting little boys after being tormented by one? Or did your dog suddenly begin soiling the house when you brought a new puppy into the household? Either of these events can cause your dog to misbehave if he does not feel secure in his own environment. Maintaining your basic obedience training will help your pet feel secure regardless of what happens around him.

Many older dogs will not relax into the enjoyment of doing obedience work in the same manner as younger ones. They have been doing things their own way for a while and may not be willing to give up their position in the hierarchy. This is especially true of dogs that are aggressive toward visitors or intimidate their owners by growling or snapping. This is behavior that has formed gradually over a period of time without being checked.

Most of the dogs that I have seen having the behavior problem of aggression toward visitors and/or their owners are upward of four years old. These dogs may have begun to exhibit this behavior as young adults. When they found that people hesitated or jumped back when being presented with this behavior, such dogs learned that they could easily intimidate in order to show dominance. The owners of these dogs would unconsciously encourage such behavior—when their dog was going after a visitor—by coddling, using a tight lead, or putting the dog into confinement; or—when the dog jumped, by petting on command; or—when the dog chewed the new shoe—by letting the dog keep it. All of which added to the problem.

The best method of curing this misbehavior is to make your dog work throughout the time there are visitors (or family members if the dog goes after certain people) present. For example, if your dog likes to bite people as they are leaving, place your dog in a sit or down/stay when the person gets up to leave. If you have a dog that chases and bites children as they run and play in your yard, then teach your dog to remain in a down/stay whenever there are children present.

Basic Obedience

As you can see, the best cure for most misbehaviors is basic obedience. If you can train your dog to work for you on and off the lead regardless of distractions, then you can overcome almost any behavior problem.

When you begin training your elderly dog, keep in mind his hardheadedness, and be sure that you maintain your own persistence. While some dogs will give in quickly and begin enjoying themselves, even if they are ten years old, others will not be very happy when they see the training collar come out. Be prepared for this reaction! It does not always mean that you are teaching your pet incorrectly. It is simply that he does not appreciate being put in a lower position in the hierarchy after being "king of the house" for so long.

Special Needs

While some elderly dogs are in full sensory awareness, there are others that have lost their eyesight or hearing due to advanced age. If this is the case with your dog, there are several training methods that can be successful.

Training a Deaf Dog

Let's first explore the methods for training a deaf dog. While he does not hear your vocal tones, he still sees your visual cues, and feels vibrations through the ground and air. He will also feel the tug of a collar. (I recommend using a regular buckle collar on this dog—provided he is elderly. If you are training a large adolescent dog that is deaf, then stay with the training collar.)

Utilizing the senses of which your dog is capable, do the following:

1. Begin the training of your dog inside your house. You can get stronger ground vibrations on an interior floor than on the grass or tarmac outside.

2. Make all your praise physical. Scratch your pet in his favorite places when he performs well.

3. When reprimanding your dog, use a tug on the collar as you stomp your foot.

4. If you are having a difficult time getting your dog's attention, use food to bait him, as you would with a young puppy.

The rest of the training should follow much as it would for a normal dog. You should be consistent and clear in all of your communications. Be sure that your visual cues are very different from each other, and utilize your whole body to communicate your desires. For example, when teaching your dog to come, crouch down and tap the floor. When he is coming to you, feel your pleasure as well as showing it in the smile on your face. Your dog will pick up on your positive emotions. The petting and praise when your dog arrives should be enthusiastic to encourage the behavior. Your dog will soon learn that as soon as he sees you crouch down you wish for him to come.

Training a Blind Dog

Training a blind dog is no more difficult than working with one that is deaf. Use your vocal cues instead of your visual ones. Most blind dogs make their way with the use of their enhanced hearing capabilities. Dogs can hear the echoes off objects and the direction and distance of a sound. Their incredible use of scent is also extremely helpful.

I recommend spending much time with your dog in a safe place where your dog knows the whereabouts and smells of all the objects, so that he most easily learns the different tones of your voice. Sit on the floor with him and speak in soothing tones, giving him treats now and then.

Begin by teaching him to sit. Use the same tones of voice that you use on a normal dog, and place him in position. As soon as he is sitting, give him a lot of praise and petting. Continue your training in the same manner as you would a very young puppy. Use a lot of coaxing, and praise. If your dog is not responding to the praise, then use the food bait to key him in to walking with you or coming to the sound of your voice. Be sure that when you do call him to come there are not any objects or obstructions in his path to you.

Many dogs will feel more secure if they can be touching you. Allow your dog to lean into you, or to bump against you now and then. This is similar to what blind people do with their seeing-eye dogs. In this situation you have become a seeing-eye person for your dog.

Some dogs that cannot see will become frightened at certain smells and sounds. You can overcome this with the same type of distraction-proofing you would do with a normal dog. Simply work your pet through the situations that frighten him. He will learn from your confidence that there is nothing to be upset about.

Training a Dog with a Physical Disability

Another disability that can sometimes make training difficult or cause a breakdown of training is a physical problem. Many elderly dogs will begin to exhibit house soiling, chewing, or even aggression due to a physical malfunction. Be sure that you rule out any physiological problem before you begin your training sessions.

6. Housebreaking

THE EASIEST METHOD of housebreaking any dog or puppy is through crate training. The crate can be used as a place where your puppy/dog can feel secure and maintain positive associations. Most dogs will not mess in their sleeping area, thus encouraging control until let outside to an appropriate area.

Mosby, standing in his wire crate.

If you do not own a crate, you can use a kitchen or bathroom closed off with baby gates. Keep in mind, however, that a bored dog will chew and may get into trouble if kept for a long period in the enclosure. The area in which you keep your puppy should be warm and near the center of your household activity. Dogs are social animals and are happier when near their family pack.

The ideal situation for housebreaking is to be with the puppy at all times. If you are able to arrange to do this, then proceed as follows:

If you follow these directions, you can housebreak your puppy within a week. The most important aspect of this procedure is to keep your eyes on your puppy at all times. If you look away for a few seconds, then your puppy may make a mess.

The correction for these mistakes should be swift and firm. Be certain to do it in a way that your dog will understand. Do not yell, scream, or smack him. Simply grab him firmly by the scruff of his neck, drag him—or carry him by the scruff—to the mess, place his nose next to it as you say "No!" in a low, scary tone of voice, and then push him away from you. Do not pet or play with him for at least a half hour. Dogs hate being ignored.

If you cannot remain home with your puppy, then the housebreaking may take longer but can still be done. You must keep him in a crate or enclosed area at all times while you are away. The ideal situation is an exercise pen with his bed on one side and the entire surface covered with newspaper. If you have outdoor facilities, then you will have an easier time. However, if you must keep him indoors and contained for over five hours, it is only fair to assume that your puppy must relieve himself during that time. A large crate can also be sectioned off into a sleep area and a relief area.

As your puppy grows he will be able to hold himself for a longer period. You can remove the newspapers eventually and expect that he will not relieve himself in his enclosure.

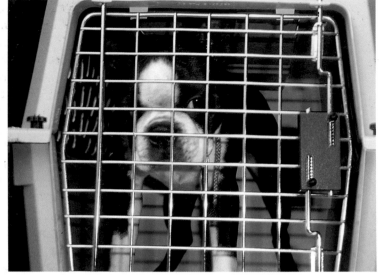

Daisy, standing in her plastic crate.

When you are home, be sure to keep him out of his enclosure as much as possible. Keep your eyes on him at all times, letting him outside on a regular basis.

Overcoming a Housebreaking Problem

If you are trying to overcome a housebreaking problem then the procedures are somewhat different. Let's assume that the problem is with a dog over six months of age, because, if your dog is not housebroken by this time, it is a behavior problem. Once again, he should be confined while you are away, and watched when you are home. A dog that insists on relieving himself in your house does so for a particular reason, such as not respecting you as the alpha figure, or simply because he has not been taught correctly. Many dogs who do not respect their owners will urinate in front of them. Other dogs may be sneaky about it by going out of sight and then messing. Generally the sneaky dogs understand that it is wrong to mess in the house, but are being stubborn about trying to become the alpha figure. The dogs that urinate in front of their owners simply have no regard for those owners, or may have a physical problem. (If this becomes a persistent problem, I recommend that you consult your veterinarian. The source of the problem could be anything from an internal infection to the wrong type of food.)

The punishment for being a sneaky dog should be similar to your reprimand for a puppy messing, but is taken one step further. That step is called isolation treatment.

You will first reprimand the dog in the same manner that you would ordinarily reprimand another canine; then you use some social psychology by putting the dog in a small dark place for a half hour. Each time your dog is bad he will receive this treatment with increased isolation time. (I recommend against using his crate or confined quarters for his isolation treatment.) If your dog messes in your living room while you are in the kitchen, you should punish your dog as soon as you find the mess. (Yes, dogs do remember.)

First of all, do not call your dog to you. Go to him. Grab him by the scruff of the neck, drag or carry him to the mess, place his nose next to it—not in it—and say "No!" in a low, scary tone of voice as you shake him. Then, drag or carry him to the isolation area, place him inside, and shut the door. Leave him inside for a half hour. Each time you must repeat this reprimand for the same type of mess, add ten minutes onto the previous isolation time. Your dog will look very droopy when you let him out. Continue to ignore him for another fifteen minutes. If your dog begins to howl, or scratch at the door of the isolation chamber, then open the door, lunge at the dog as you say "No!" and shut the door. Do this every time he begins making noise or scratching. Remember to be consistent if you want your dog to listen to you.

Schedule 1

5:30 – 6:00 a.m.	Take him outside
6:15 a.m.	Feed him
6:30 a.m.	Take him outside

During the day take him outside every two hours, and after he sleeps, plays, or works.

4 p.m.	Feed him
4:15 p.m.	Take him outside

During the evening take him outside every two hours, especially after playing or working.

10 p.m.	Take him outside
	(for his last relief time)

Upon returning inside, place him in his enclosure (crate), for the night. You can also put him there if you cannot watch him at any time during the day.

Schedule 2

5:30 – 6:00 a.m.	Take him outside
6:15 a.m.	Feed him
6:30 a.m.	Take him outside, and work or play
	(for at least 20 minutes)

Place your pet in a crate or enclosure while you are at work. If the dog is to be in this area for more than five hours, arrange for someone to let him out at midday. Either a neighbor or dog walker would be sufficient to allow your pet a chance to relieve himself and stretch his legs.

5:00 p.m.	Immediately take him outside
5:30 p.m.	Feed him
5:45 p.m.	Take out, work or play with him
	(for at least an hour)

Keep him with you the rest of the evening, taking him out every two hours. When you go to bed, put him back in the enclosure. When your pet proves able to contain himself all night, keep him enclosed in your bedroom with you. He'll be unlikely to mess or be destructive in your presence, and will be grateful to be with you instead of being locked up.

Some dogs will form a guilty conscience while learning the do's and don'ts of your household. Your dog knows that his action was wrong and will hide to avoid inevitable punishment. I consider this one of the many "tricks" that dogs pull. They show guilt in hopes of not receiving the reprimand. Don't fall for it! You must be firm about your criterion. Do not, however, reprimand your dog as soon as you return home. If you were to do this, he would not look forward to your return; he would be frightened. Always greet your dog with enthusiasm upon your return, regardless of how guilty he looks. After greeting your dog and taking him outside, then you can take a moment to observe your surroundings. If a mess has been made, your dog must be punished accordingly. Keeping your dog in his crate or enclosure when you are not home will avoid all of this unpleasantness.

Sample Schedules

Adjacent are two sample schedules for housebreaking. The first entails training a dog if you work in the home, and the second if you work out of the home.

Telling You He Needs to Go Out

Dogs vary in their means of communicating their need to relieve themselves. In order to understand what your dog is trying to convey, you will either need to be very observant or to teach him a way to let you know.

Some dogs will sit patiently at the door, others will bark, and some will sit quietly watching you. A clear signal is your pet sniffing the floor and walking in a circle. This is a sure sign of impending doom. It is almost too late to change fate.

Be aware of your dog at all times. If he displays any of these behaviors, immediately ask him, "Do you want to go outside?" Sound excited, causing him to pick up on the exuberance of the moment. Immediately take him out. If he does his business, praise him. If not, wait awhile until he does. The exercise is likely to make him go.

The surest means of teaching your dog to let you know he must go outside is to give him the means of communicating this to you. Teach him to ring a bell to let you know.

Teaching your dog to perform this trick will not only be fun, but also functional.

• Hang a cowbell from the doorknob of the exit to your pet's potty area. Make sure it's low enough for your pet to reach it easily.

• Every time before going out, rub a little soft cheese on the bell, so your dog will lick it off, causing the bell to ring.

• Pair the word "Outside" with the sound of the bell. Praise your pet as he makes it move.

• Be consistent about going out the same door and using this technique every time.

Within a week or two you can phase out the use of cheese as your dog learns the association between the sound of the bell and going outside.

Passive Submission Problems

Many puppies and older dogs have a problem called submissive urination. This is not a breach of your housebreaking rules. It is called passive submission, a reaction to a dominant stimulus, usually male, due to the lower tone of voice. Sometimes just excitement can cause this reaction in puppies. They become so excited that they cannot control their ureter or sphincter muscles.

Do not punish your puppy or older dog for this behavior. You will only make it worse. It will help if you greet your dog in a crouched position, thus decreasing his anxiety instead of frightening him. If your dog reacts to certain people with this submissive action, ask those people not to go toward him; let the dog go to the person when he is ready, and sniff him/her without being touched. Most puppies and dogs will overcome this reaction, so be patient.

If your dog is not housebroken within several weeks, then it is time to consult a professional dog trainer. Usually a basic obedience course will straighten out the situation. Teaching your dog to listen goes hand in hand with solving any behavior problem.

7. The Heel

TRAINING YOUR DOG to heel requires somewhat different techniques depending on the age and development of your pet. A young puppy has capabilities and needs that differ from those of an older puppy or adult dog.

Training a Puppy 2–4 Months

You must be careful not to traumatize a young pup, or he will not enjoy working. I will sometimes use a small piece of food to coax the puppy into doing things. There are some puppies that do not care what delicious object you have in your hand; they will simply be stubborn. These stubborn puppies require more patience and persistence than the "food hounds."

Begin your pup's first lesson by getting him used to wearing a collar. The collar can be a choke chain (as long as it is not in the choke mode) or a regular buckle collar. Play with your puppy as he wears it so that his mind is not entirely on the strange object around his neck. Once he is used to the collar, attach the leash to it and let him drag it around for a while. Never let your puppy chew on the leash. This can be the start of a bad habit and can get pretty expensive, as you must keep replacing leashes. If your pup puts the leash in his mouth, jerk it out as you say "No!" Replace the bad thing with a good one. Give him a toy, and play with him as you praise him.

Show your puppy the food as you give the heel command, and step forward on your left leg.

How You Should Proceed

If your puppy is a big "food hound," do the following:

1. Put the leash in your right hand, and little bits of food in your left hand.

2. As you say your dog's name and the command "Heel," step forward with your left leg.

3. Coax your puppy to your left leg with the food. When he arrives, give him the treat, and praise him.

4. Do this a few times; then do two steps. By this time your puppy will figure out that he must follow you to receive the treat.

5. When you can go ten to fifteen steps forward, begin to do turns as your pup follows along. When you do your first couple of turns, stop right after each turn to give your pup his reward.

At no point should you have to tug on the lead. It should remain loose at your left side. Your puppy is cueing in on the treat and eventually on you.

After practicing with this exercise for a few days you can begin to phase out the treats. Begin by giving your pup the food every other time he heels, and then every two times. Gradually, make it irregular intervals, so that he does not know when he will or will not receive the food. Within several training sessions you will find that you are able to limit his treats to after a training exercise.

If you begin working your pup around distractions, you will need to begin reprimanding him when he is out of the heel position. The best way to obtain your pup's attention is to do a turn. He will automatically receive a tug on the lead as you turn. Be sure to say "No!" as you make the turn, and resume the praise as your pup returns to your side. You will need to constantly guide your puppy with your voice. The whole time he is good, praise him enthusiastically. When he is not with you (i.e., his right shoulder even with your left leg), say "No!" in a low tone and give the leash a quick, firm tug. Do not pull on the leash. Pulling will only frighten him and make him pull in the opposite direction.

Once you no longer need the food to keep him with you, the leash position changes. Now you should hold the loop of the lead in your right hand, and grab the lead midway down with your left hand. There should be a loop in the lead between you and your pup. Your left hand should be holding the lead palm down, your hand at your side. This position allows you to give firm, quick tugs without injuring yourself or pulling on your pup's neck.

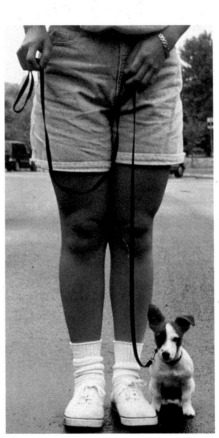

The proper heel position. The dog's right shoulder is even with his owner's left leg.

If you have a puppy who is not a food hound, then you must be more persistent with your discipline. The more stubborn puppy will require you, too, to be stubborn. This does not mean you must be harsh; just remain patient and strive to attain your goals in smaller intervals.

1. Let your pup get used to the collar and lead as I described previously.

2. As you give the "Heel" command and take the first step forward with your left leg, immediately crouch down and coax your puppy to you. When he arrives, give him loads of praise and petting in his favorite spots (such as his tummy). Continue in this manner for the full session, which should last about ten minutes.

3. The next session, take two steps at a time. Gradually increase the amount of steps you take as your pup accedes to your directions. If he tries to go in the opposite direction, give the lead a firm tug, and say "No!" He may try to back away from you. Some pups will even do flips and whine out of frustration. You must remain firm and bring him back to your side. I understand that it can be difficult to withstand this behavior, but if you don't, you will have a dog that takes *you* for a walk.

Keep all training sessions short, and play with your pup afterward. You will accomplish more with short, frequent sessions—such as ten minutes three times a day—than with a half hour at one time. A puppy has a short attention span and low tolerance to stress. These must be built up gradually; so don't push it.

Distraction-proofing during the figure-eight exercise. Using dogs as obstructions (posts) as well as distractions in the surrounding area will help to proof a dog into listening at all times.

Proper heeling position. The dog is on your left side, its right shoulder even with your left leg. The dog is attentive, awaiting your command.

Training an Older Puppy 4–6 Months

Although it may seem easier to train a pup at this age by virtue of its longer attention span and better tolerance to stress, it does not make the same impression on the dog at this age as it does on one that is younger. When you train a young pup you are essentially beginning with a clean slate and are forming its future behavior. An older pup, however, has already learned a few bad habits and must be retrained, instead of simply shown the proper behavior. By six months a dog has formed his personality, just as a child at the age of six years has formed his. You will find the older pup will be more easily distracted and far more energetic, constantly testing his surroundings and vying for the top-dog position.

You must go about the training of the heel with diligence and persistence. Do not give in to your dog's stopping to sniff or lunging toward a distraction. Remain calm, positive, and firm.

1. Begin by allowing your pup to get used to the choke chain and lead as you would with a younger pup. Small dogs such as miniature breeds will not require a choke chain.

2. Hold your leash as described previously (loop in right hand, left hand palm down midway down the lead). Put any extra lead into your right hand.

3. Begin by saying your dog's name and the command "Heel!" in an authoritative tone. Do not repeat the command. Step forward on your left leg as you give the command.

Your pup may be wandering around you sniffing as you begin. Slap your left leg as you take those forward steps. This sound will obtain your pup's attention. As he looks at you, praise him.

4. Continue walking a few steps; then stop, say "Break," and crouch down. Pet and praise him exuberantly.

5. After about twenty seconds, begin your heel again. Gradually increase the distance you walk in between each break time. Always praise your pup when he is with you, and give him a quick, firm snap on the lead with a "No!" if he is not. Turning frequently will increase his attentiveness. Another means of doing this is changing your pace.

If your pup should lag, use the sound of slapping your left leg along with an encouraging tone of voice to make him catch up to you. Do not pull him to you. This would only intimidate him.

6. After about fifteen minutes, end the session. Your pup will be very tired. Allow him at least a half hour to himself in his enclosure (or yard). You can also give him a treat after his session.

Heel. Begin walking on your left leg as you tell your dog to heel.

You can gradually build on your pup's attention span and tolerance as you continue to work him. When he shows signs of being tired, such as continued lagging or trying to lie down, make him work just a few more minutes before stopping the session. In the next lesson he will be able to tolerate more work. It would be prudent not to overwork your pup or he will not like his training sessions.

Teaching a Dog over Six Months of Age

The methods for teaching the older dog are similar to those for the older puppy; however, you will be working with an animal that is not only stronger but harder-headed. He will try to pull or stop you when he wants to sniff. Some have devised several "tricks" to get their way. These tricks include jumping up on you, biting at the lead, plowing (putting his head down and pulling), or planting himself and not moving no matter how hard you pull. You must overcome these tricks by being persistent and maintaining your own pace no matter what your dog tries to do.

Overcoming Clever "Tricks"

You will need to do many turns at the outset. For example, when you give the heel command you will need to turn in the opposite direction within a few steps. You will find yourself turning constantly at first. After several minutes of this you will be able to take more and more steps in one direction before having to turn. As soon as your dog looks up at you, praise him, say "Break," crouch down, and pet him. After twenty seconds of break time give your heel command again. Always praise your dog the whole time he is in the proper position, and say "No!" as you snap the lead when he is not. Try not to give a snap with the command. This will make a bad association with the command.

If your dog tries any of the above-mentioned tricks do the following:

Jumping up—Jerk your dog with your "No!" reprimand in the opposite direction of his jump. For example, he is jumping on your left side as you walk. Say "No!" and jerk him in the opposite direction, toward *his* left. If he is jumping on you from behind, jerk him forward toward your left leg as he jumps. Do not stop walking; this will only reinforce the bad behavior.

Biting the lead—Snap the lead out of his mouth. As you continue walking simply snap the lead firmly with your "No!" reprimand tone. Repeat as necessary.

Plowing—Turn in the opposite direction, as you snap the lead and walk quickly. Every time his nose goes down do a turn. If you can time the turn to occur just as your dog's nose begins to go down, you will have an easier time with the action—as well as with stopping the behavior entirely in a more timely manner.

Planting—This can be very difficult to correct if you have already given in to it for a long time. Your dog will know your frustration threshold and will hold out until you reach it. Ne-ver give in first. When you give the heel command, keep going, even if it means dragging the dog behind you. You will find that your dog will not appreciate being dragged for too long and will find that life is much more pleasant when walking at your side. This behavior will be quickly overcome if you are more stubborn about it than your dog.

The left about-turn. If the dog gets a little ahead, the left about-turn should be applied. You should take a big step with the left leg, and turn into the dog with your right leg, effectively shoving him aside. Most dogs will fall back into place after this type of turn.

Effective Turns

The right turn is most effective when your dog is very far ahead of you, is sniffing, or is more than six inches from your left leg. When you do turn, do so quickly without warning or hesitation. Do not drag your dog behind you. Snap the lead to-ward your belly as you turn, or give several snaps. Always say "No!" if the turn is a reprimand.

The left turn is most effective if your dog is by your side but tends to get a few inches ahead of your left leg. This turn is the most effective heeling reprimand that you can do. It does not require any snapping, and teaches your dog to keep a close eye on you.

As you see your dog inching ahead of you, take a big step with your left leg and swing your right leg ahead of your dog. You may have to push at your dog with your legs as you turn. A large dog may require a firm shove with your knees into his neck as you turn. Dogs hate being bumped and will be very watchful of where your legs are so that it does not happen often. A distracted dog, however, will not care as much about it, so you will need to do circles to the left until your dog begins to watch where you are going.

Heeling with a Halti. Phantom is wearing a Halti head collar. It is not a muzzle! The Halti guides a dog's head, similarly to a horse halter. It is completely painless, and helps in training a large and strong dog.

Heeling with the Halti

While your vocal tones and visual cues are exactly the same as when you use a choke chain, the leash movement while using a Halti will be entirely different. To understand how to train with this device you must first know the principle behind its design.

Dr. Roger Mugford borrowed the principles of leading large animals. Have you ever seen a horse or cow led with a collar around its neck? No, they wear halters. These halters enable a person who weighs less than 10 percent of a horse or cow to control the larger animal without being pulled along if the animal wishes to go somewhere. All it requires is a firm tug in a downward motion to stop the horse from pulling. *Voila,* you now have control without a fight.

In many ways using a Halti speeds up the training process, because the dog is constantly having to pay attention. It is far easier to stop a dog from sniffing or pulling when using this device than the regular collar or choke chain. Best of all, it causes no damage to the tender tracheal area of a canine's neck if he tries to pull. Dr. Mugford cites an example of a study in which "the 100kg tow of a St. Bernard was reduced to less than 2kgs on the Halti." It works! I've been more successful using this device on a large, pulling dog than I could ever have accomplished with a pinch collar. The major plus is, I didn't have to hurt the animals (as a pinch collar would) in order to obtain the proper responses.

Another company to follow closely the design of the Dr. Mugford's Halti is Ameri-Pet, Inc., which manufactures the Gentle Leader. This is also an efficient training tool. While it operates much the same as the Halti, it uses less material, and thus may be more comfortable for the dog.

You will find that as soon as you put the Halti on your dog, he will either become very subdued or will frantically try to get it off. Putting something on his face for the first time might be compared to your trying on a new pair of shoes that don't fit as comfortably as sneakers. Your pet will try pulling it off with a forepaw, rubbing his face on the ground, opening his mouth as wide as possible, and even throwing himself around. This is to be expected.

To teach acceptance of the Halti, have treats available. Give him a treat as he sits calmly or stops fussing with the Halti. The food reward will also help you get started without having to pull his mouth shut. Approach the training of the heel just as you would with a young puppy. Give your pet a treat every time you stop.

Remembering that the Halti was derived from the halters for large farm animals, keep in mind the direction you need to pull in order to get your dog's attention—to override the wonderful smells or the cute poodle walking on the other side of the road. Pull down!

Teaching your dog to heel with the Halti goes quickly:

1. Attach your leash to the ring under his chin.

2. Hold your leash as you would with the other collar, but a little tighter between you and your pet. Allow approximately 8 inches (20 cm) of leash between your left hand and the Halti.

3. Begin by saying your dog's name and the command "Heel."

Proper heeling position with a Halti. The dog's ears are even with your left leg.

4. Take your first step with your left leg, as you hold a treat directly under his nose.

5. Move forward only five steps before stopping and giving him the treat, as you praise him.

6. Repeat, increasing your steps between every stop.

As long as you tug and release instead of constantly pull, your pet will learn how to heel within about fifteen minutes.

Although the directions enclosed with the Halti and Gentle Leader say to pull up and back if your dog gets ahead, I find this causes more of a struggle, and less response. I recommend that you always pull *down* and in the opposite direction from your dog's pull. If he forges ahead of you, pull down and back. If he heels wide, pull down and toward you. If he lags behind because of a distraction, pull down and forward. This pulling down puts pressure on his upper nose, instead of closing his mouth as would occur with an upward tug.

Your dog will quickly tire, especially on a first training session. If he begins to lag, coax him to you by placing all the leash in your right hand and by slapping your leg with your left as you say, "Come on!" in an excited tone of voice.

If your dog persists in trying to get the Halti off, try leaving it on during the times you are with him but not working. If he sees he can still eat, drink, and play while wearing it, he will accept it better for training.

If your dog plants himself as you walk, pull down and forward on the leash.

If your dog forges ahead while heeling, pull down and back on the leash. The tug should be quick and firm, releasing the pressure immediately.

8. The Sit

Once you have your dog watching you attentively as you walk with him, you can begin training him to sit. You can do this exercise as you heel or as you interact with your dog. If you wish to begin teaching your dog to sit as part of your interaction, then do the following:

1. Place one hand on your dog's chest and the other on his rear.

2. As you say his name and the command "Sit!" put simultaneous pressure at both points, (i.e., press downward on his rear as you push him back on his chest).

3. As soon as his rear end touches the floor (or ground, if outside), release the body pressure and praise him exuberantly.

4. Repeat this procedure often.

If you wish to teach your dog to sit in conjunction with the heel, there are several different methods. The method you use de-pends on the age of your dog. If you are working with a young puppy, you can use food treats, or if your dog is older than four or five months, you can use the push-down method. These methods vary according to the situations in which they are used.

Keeping the treat directly in front of your puppy's nose, lift it over his head so that he looks up. As he looks up, his rear end goes down.

No matter which method you wind up using, your dog should always sit facing in the same direction that you are facing, his right shoulder even with your left leg.

The Sit with a Puppy

First, I will explain the method used for teaching a young puppy to sit.

Begin your training session just as you have been doing with your heeling exercises. As you stop, do the following:

1. Hold the treat in your left hand just over your pup's nose, so that he can smell it but cannot eat it.

2. As you stop, say his name and the command "Sit!"

3. As he looks up at the treat, move it slowly toward his rear but still just up over his nose. As he looks at it, his rear end will drop. When it does, praise him, and give him the treat.

4. As soon as he eats it, go directly into your heel.

5. Each time you stop, tell him to sit as you hold the treat over his head.

6. After several repetitions begin to phase out the treats, just as you did with the heel exercise.

The Sit with an Older Puppy or Dog

If you are working with a dog over four months old, then I recommend using the following method when teaching your dog to sit while doing the heel exercise.

1. Take your dog forward in the heel. Before you stop, take up the slack in the leash as follows:

2. Place your right hand parallel to your left on the leash.

3. Grip the leash with your right hand, without letting go with your left. Slide your left hand down to your left thigh, and "glue" your hand to your thigh, gripping the leash.

4. Now stop. After you have stopped, say your dog's name and the command "Sit!" only one time.

The sit. The dog should sit in the same position as it heels, its right shoulder even with your left leg.

Begin the heel exercise by moving forward on your left leg first, as you give the heel command.

Preparing to stop. The leash is gathered, making it tighter just moments before stopping. The left hand should be "glued" to the left leg as you stop, thus preventing the dog from continuing on.

5. As you give the command, place the leash in your right hand, keeping it "glued" to your left thigh, and bring your left hand onto your dog's lower back, just above the hip bones.

6. Press gently into the muscles of your dog's lower back, in the hollows above his hip bones.

7. As soon as your dog is in the sit position praise him, and take him into the heel.

8. Repeat the exercise every 5 to 10 steps. It is also helpful to do it directly after a turn. This increases your dog's attentiveness.

9. After several sessions of placing your dog, as you give the command begin to hesitate for about five seconds before placing him. He may have an understanding of the exercise and do the sit without your having to place him. If he does not do so after the five seconds, place him and then praise him once he is in position.

Placing the dog into the sit. First, transfer the entire leash into the right hand, which should be "glued" to the left leg. This leaves your left hand free to gently push just above the hip bones.

Dealing with a Stubborn Dog

Do not worry if your dog does not pick up this command right away. Some dogs can be very stubborn about this, especially if they are older than five months.

If after four days of consistent work your dog still refuses to sit on command, then you should proceed with the following:

1. Gather the lead before stopping, as you have done previously.

2. Upon stopping, say your dog's name and the command "Sit!"

3. Give your dog five seconds to comply; if he does not, then with your release of his collar snap up firmly and quickly as you say "No!" in a low tone. Release the collar as quickly as you snapped up.

4. If he does not sit, then repeat the upward snap up to four times. Each snap should be firmer and each successive "No!" in a lower tone of voice.

5. Most dogs will feel cowed by that action and will sit; if not, then re-place the dog with the muscle pressure, and snap an additional time the next time you work on this.

6. As soon as your dog sits, be sure that you release your tight hold on the lead and at the same time praise him exuberantly.

I have worked with several dogs that this action only makes more stubborn about not doing the sit. If you have tried this reprimand for several days and are unsuccessful or your dog begins to show aggression, then do the following:

1. As you give the sit command, pull upward and back on the lead, choking your dog into the sit position. Your dog will be stubborn the first few times but has no choice. He must sit. He will require less and less pulling pressure as you repeat the exercise. Eventually he will give in and sit on command.

2. This procedure avoids asserting overt aggression toward the dog—and avoids your getting any in return. Unfortunately the dog will have to be choked briefly, but you will get your point across.

3. Be certain that you release the choke chain as soon as he sits and at the same time give him lots of praise.

Teaching the Sit with a Halti

Begin by teaching the sit as you would with a young puppy. The treat you used to make him move forward in the heel will now be used to make him sit before he receives it. Hold it above his head slightly as you give the "Sit" command. Praise him when he sits.

If your dog does not sit on command, you will need to place him in position in the following manner:

1. As you stop, take the entire leash into your right hand, less than three inches from its ring attachment on the collar.

2. Bring your right hand directly in front of your dog's nose once you are stopped.

3. As you give him the sit command, pull up directly under his chin.

Perform a correction for not sitting on command by pulling up on the Halti, directly under your dog's chin, as you push gently in the hollows above his hip bones.

4. As soon as your dog attains the sit position, release the pressure on the Halti and praise him. You can also give him a treat if you wish.

You will find that your dog will quickly pick up the sit exercise if you follow these directions. Be sure that you do not maintain a pull on your dog's nose after he sits. This can be detrimental to the entire training process.

The Automatic Sit

The criterion for this behavior consists of the dog sitting whenever and wherever you stop while heeling. Your dog's shoulder should be even with your left leg and he should be facing the same direction as you. Do not let your standard slip for any reason, whether you are opening a door or fence gate, or stopping to speak with a neighbor. The dog must *always* sit when you stop, without your having to give the command.

You'll know your dog is ready for this exercise when he begins sitting as soon as you stop—before you give him the command to do so. Most will do this naturally, for they pick up on patterns quickly, and want to please you. Some may be inconsistent with the reaction, due to being distracted at a given time when you stop.

Your dog will be ready for you to reinforce the automatic sit when you see him sitting automatically about 80 percent of the time. To reinforce this behavior do the following:

1. Begin your training session in the heel.

2. Before you stop, gather your leash as I have previously described.

3. Be sure that your left hand remains on your left thigh when stopped. If your hand is on your thigh, then your dog has no choice but to stop and remain at your side.

4. If your dog does not sit automatically within about five seconds, then snap upward on the lead as you say "No!"

5. I doubt you'll have to snap more than a few times. As soon as your dog sits, praise him and go directly into the heel again.

Practice this exercise in front of distractions of all sorts, such as people, other animals, and your pet's toys. The ultimate training goal is to have your animal listen in all situations. To attain this goal you cannot avoid any distraction. You must confront it and work your dog through it in a consistent manner. I will discuss distraction-proofing after you have learned how to do the stay exercise in Chapter 9, which follows.

Once you have a foothold on doing the heel, sit, and stay, you will be able to control your dog as he is exposed to distractions. The entire groundwork will be laid out, and you will know how to be consistent and persistent. And above all, give your dog lots of praise whenever he does well.

9. The Stay

Before beginning this exercise, you must decide on your goals. Do you want your dog to remain in one spot for however long you wish, or do you only want him to remain temporarily? I feel that it is best to teach a dog to remain indefinitely until released, regardless of the situation. To attain this goal you will have to be very consistent and disciplined with your criterion. Your dog should remain in the spot in which he was told to stay. Don't allow him to change the direction he is facing; nor should he be allowed to lie down on a sit/stay. If you allow him to do either of the aforementioned things, your dog will not be reliable on the stay exercise.

Training the Puppy

You will discover that teaching a young puppy to stay will require a lot of patience, repetition, and consistency. Keep in mind that your puppy has a very short attention span but is very receptive to your directions. You can teach your pup the stay through the play training or while you do your heeling work.

Teaching a stay during the round-robin puppy game. Crouch down, and give the signal as soon as your puppy sits. Maintain your signal as you praise your pup; then give him a treat.

If you do this during the playtime, be sure to have him cueing in on your hand when you give the stay signal. Since he has previously been trained with food treats, he will most likely respond to hand movements.

1. Give your pup the sit command. As soon as he sits, praise him.

2. Place either hand—be sure always to use that same hand—in front of his face. You should spread your fingers wide, with the palm facing him. This makes a large visual cue.

3. Say your pup's name and the command "Stay."

4. If he tries getting up, say, "No!" Place him back in the same position, and repeat your command. There will be a lot of this at first. Remain persistent.

5. Make him stay longer with each successive stay command.

6. Remain directly in front of him until he is reliable enough to stay for about thirty seconds.

If you are training your pup to stay during your heeling exercises do the following:

1. Begin with a few minutes of heeling and sit exercises.

2. When your puppy is "warmed up," begin at the sit.

3. Take all of the leash in your left hand.

4. Bring your right hand in front of your puppy's face (not from the front, but from the side), using the same open-palm signal.

5. As you present the signal, say your pup's name and the command "Stay!"

6. As your pup remains in position, praise him.

7. If he gets up, say, "No!" Replace him in the sit position, and repeat both your visual and verbal commands.

Stand in front of your puppy with the leash over his head in a straight line. Be sure to praise him as he remains in his sit.

Step out on your right foot first, as you give the stay signal and command.

Once your puppy sits at your side, place your right hand in front of his face as you give the stay command.

8. After presenting your signal and command, step out right foot first and pivot in front of your pup. Remain in front of him for gradual-ly increasing increments on each stay command.

9. As you remain facing your dog, hold the leash up over his head, with the collar loose.

Remember not to repeat your command. Do not continually say "Stay!" Say it only once when presenting your visual signal, or any time you must replace your pup into the sit/stay position.

Training the Older Puppy or Dog

The procedures are similar to training a puppy while doing the heeling exercises; however, you can be firmer and do leash reprimands if your dog does not remain in position.

1. Give the stay command just as you would for the puppy.

The stay. Put all of the leash into the left hand. Show the dog the signal as you give the stay command.

2. Always step forward with your right leg after (or during) giving the stay command with the visual signal.

The stay. Step forward on your right leg, as you give both the verbal and visual commands.

3. You should be standing upright in front of your dog. The whole time he remains in the sit/stay be sure to praise him; if he gets up at any time, then he must be reprimanded immediately.

The stay. Stand directly in front of your dog, with the collar completely loose and the leash over your dog's head in a straight line from the collar to your hand. You must remain standing upright as the dog receives praise.

4. To reprimand, use the same upward leash snap as you did when your dog would not sit on command. Say "No!" with each snap. Be sure that each snap is firmer than the previous one, and that each "No!" is said with the snap in a lower tone—not louder.

5. Once your dog returns himself to the sit position, give him the stay command again.

6. Gradually increase each stay until your dog can remain in place for up to one minute.

I call the next phase of the sit/stay the "Elongation of the Stay." This involves moving around your dog. He should be able to remain in one place

If your dog lies down while he is supposed to be sitting, grab the back of the collar, and lift him into a sit. If this causes your dog to roll onto his back, go directly into a heel for only one or two steps, and begin the sit exercise over again.

as you walk all of the way around him. Be sure to keep your lead above his head in case he tries to get up. This will ensure a quick response if he does try to get up.

1. Begin by shuffling back and forth in front of your dog as he stays.

The elongated stay. Once the dog can remain in a stay position for a minute, begin moving around side to side in front as you continue to praise him.

The elongated stay. When the dog is accepting of your movement in front, the next step is to walk along each side.

2. On the next stay command move forward and back along your dog's sides.

3. Successively increase your movement with each stay command. By the fifth stay command you should be able to walk all the way around your dog.

Sit/stay. The dog should remain in one spot as you walk entirely around him.

4. After several stays in which you are walking around him, begin increasing your distance. You can begin letting out your lead so that you can go farther away. Be certain to keep your eyes on your pet so that you can be quick to reprimand if he gets up.

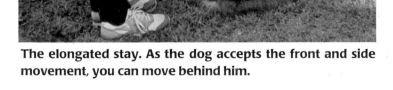

The elongated stay. As the dog accepts the front and side movement, you can move behind him.

The elongated stay. When you are able to move completely around your dog without his trying to move, gradually increase the distance as you walk.

Teaching the Stay with a Halti

Training your dog to stay in either the sit or down is almost exactly the same as when you use a regular choke chain. The only difference is that instead of jerking upward on the leash to correct the dog, you pull up under his chin until

Stay. Present your signal with your right hand as you give the stay command, and step in front of your dog with your right leg first.

Remain standing in front of your dog as he stays. Hold the leash in a straight line over his head, but not tightly. The Halti should remain loose around his muzzle.

he returns to the sit. If you are working on the stay, you first make sure the dog is sitting, and then pull downward on the Halti as you put pressure on his shoulder blades.

Please take note, however, that the aforementioned procedures are for correction only, not for use in initial training of the commands. Always give your dog a few days to learn a new word before expecting him to listen on only one command.

Distraction-Proofing

Once your pup or dog can remain in place in the stay and is walking nicely at your side, it is time to introduce him to distractions. This will teach him to be reliable in any situation. The basic idea to keep in mind is that no matter

Toys represent a great distraction-proofing opportunity.

what is going on around you, *you* should be consistent. Do not change any of your training techniques, no matter how frustrated you might get. Your dog will be looking to you for guidance; if you are distracted, you can be sure that he will also be distracted. If you can walk by people and other animals without having to look twice, then you can teach your dog to do so.

For dogs that are easily distracted, it is best to expose them *gradually* to these diversions:

1. First, expose your dog to his toys flying around. Enlist the aid of a friend or family member to throw your dog's toys around as he remains in a stay position. Once he can remain in the stay with the toys going overhead and beside him, present the distractions from all angles as he heels with you. Remember that the best way to reprimand him if he lunges for something is to quickly head in the opposite direction.

2. Once your dog will work with the flying toys, ask your helper to begin clapping his/her hands, to run and jump around, and to crouch down and slap his/her legs. Throughout these distractions your dog must remain attentive to you. If you are consistent with your standards and techniques, your dog will relax and pay attention in very little time.

3. The biggest distraction is usually another dog, or sometimes a cat. Since most people do not have a trained cat you can only take on the situation as it comes up on your walks. There are, however, many people with trained dogs or at least restrainable dogs. Try to enlist the aid of such a person in your distraction-proofing.

4. Begin your session by "warming up" your dog until he is performing all his exercises acceptably. The first exposure should be to a dog that is stationary at a distance of at least twenty feet. Once

your dog accepts that distraction and is working well in its presence, go to the next step.

5. Ask your helper to walk the distraction dog at the same distance as you continue to work your dog. You may find that your dog will react with more fervor to the other dog while it is moving.

6. When your dog settles down to working again as the other dog is moving, then it is time to bring the distraction dog closer in.

7. The best time to bring the distraction closer is while your dog remains in a sit/stay position.

8. Once your dog accepts the distraction at a closer proximity, you can begin the heel exercises.

9. While you are working your dog, the distraction dog should be alternately walking in front of and behind you. The distraction can also make passes alongside you.

10. Once your dog is accepting of this heavy distraction, you can go one more step: have the other dog *playing* as you are *working* with yours.

11. When your dog is mostly oblivious to what is going on around him, you can release him and let him go play, too.

There are several other things you can do to fully distraction-proof your dog. You can take him to parks or school yards. You can work him in front of stores in shopping plazas, or in the parking lot at a veterinarian's office. All of these situations provide a wide variety of distractions. The more places you take your dog, the better he will behave.

10. The Down

THE DOWN WILL PROBABLY be the most difficult procedure to teach your dog. From his viewpoint, it is a subordinate position. Dogs who have run things for a while will not submit to this behavior readily. You will find that puppies will not be a problem because they have not found their niche in the hierarchy yet, and are subordinate to all pack members. As in most cases, it is best to begin with a young pup, but if this is not the case, be prepared for resistance.

In normal canine socialization, when a dog lies down on its back with its tail between its legs, it is showing passive submission. Many dogs who have a generally subordinate nature may turn onto their back upon being placed down. Do not worry about how the dog lies on the floor; your criterion is simply that he is down. When your dog realizes that your command is not a negative thing, then he will adjust his position to either his haunches or his side.

Alpha shake. Look directly into the dog's eyes, as your hands grab each side of the dog's neck. Shake the dog while giving a verbal reprimand, not letting go until he looks away.

Alpha Shake

If you have a dominant dog, then he may try to growl at you or mouth your hand as you place him down. Do not allow this at any time. If your dog does this, then immediately do an alpha shake or rollover. Otherwise the growl will turn into something worse and he will refuse to go down on command as you wish. To assert your dominance and elicit his submission, do the alpha shake:

1. Grab each side of his neck.

2. Lift his front feet off the ground as you shake, and say "No!" in a low, growling tone. Be certain to look your dog in the eyes.

3. Do not stop until your dog goes limp and looks away from you or blinks.

If the alpha shake does not do the trick, then you will need to do an alpha-wolf rollover.

1. Grab your dog on each side of the neck, throw him over onto his back, stare him in the eye, and say "No!"

2. Keep him in this position until he goes limp and looks away, blinking. This is a sign of submission. Let up slowly. If he begins to struggle, then pin him again. If he remains in the submissive posture, then let him go back to what he was supposed to be doing.

Alpha rollover. Throw the dog onto its back, holding each side of its neck. Look directly into the dog's eyes as you give a verbal reprimand. Maintain this position until the dog goes limp, and looks away. When the dog gives in, slowly let go. If the dog begins to thrash around or tries to bite, then quickly repeat the exercise until you can let go slowly without the dog reacting negatively.

You can use the alpha shake and rollover for any misbehavior that your dog incurs with his mouth, or for an antijumping reprimand. I will further discuss using these maneuvers when I teach you ways that you can solve a number of behavior problems in Chapter 14 on behavior modification.

You can teach the down in conjunction with the down/stay. Your dog already knows the meaning of stay, so it will be an easy association with the new position. Doing this combination command will aid you in getting your dog to remain in position as you prepare for the heel. Give the vocal and visual commands in the same manner as you did for the sit/stay. Also use successive increments to increase your distance as your dog remains in the down.

Puppies, Small, and Submissive Dogs

There are several methods of teaching the down. For any dog—but especially for puppies, small dogs, and submissive dogs—always try the following method first in order to teach your dog the meaning of the down command. If your dog resists, then you will have to resort to one of the other methods, but always try this a few times regardless of how difficult it is to place your dog down. I have had many occasions when I had to wrestle a large dog, such as a German Shepherd or Rottweiler, into a down. I proved to the dog that I would not give in. You may have to do the same if you find yourself in this situation. Be persistent!

1. Begin your training session with your regular "warm-up" exercises, which should consist of everything that your dog has learned up to this point. Whatever you have in mind to teach your dog, you should always begin a training session with things that your dog already knows.

2. To begin the down exercise you must have your dog sitting. Be sure that your dog sits every time you stop. If this is the case, then you are ready to begin the down upon stopping.

3. Take all of the leash into your left hand. Do not hold it tightly. You should always have some slack in the lead.

4. Using your right forefinger, point downward in front of your dog's nose. Your finger can touch the ground in front of him. Sometimes tapping the ground can get him to look in that direction if he does not follow the movement.

5. As you give this visual cue, say your dog's name and the command "Down!" one time. Allow several seconds for him to look at your forefinger.

6. Then, place your left hand on your dog's shoulder blades. With your right hand get a firm hold on his forelegs. If you are working with a large dog, place your hand underneath the leg nearest you (your dog's right foreleg) and grasp his farther leg (his left foreleg).

The down. Hold the leash in your left hand. Give the signal with your right hand as you give the command.

Placing your dog in a down. Your left hand (still holding the leash) is placed on your dog's shoulder blades. Your right hand goes under the right foreleg, grabs the left foreleg, and guides both forelegs forward, as you push firmly on the shoulder blades.

7. As you bring his legs forward, put pressure on his shoulder blades with your left hand. Without this pressure your dog may raise his rear end and try to wiggle away from you.

The down. The dog should be laid gently onto the side on which you pushed him.

8. As soon as your dog's belly touches the ground, praise him and give him the stay command. Do not release the pressure on his shoulders just yet.

9. When you repeat this exercise, try to feel if there is resistance on your left hand as your dog remains in the down/stay. If so, do not let go of his shoulder blades yet. If not, then remove your hand from his shoulder blades and stand upright.

The down/stay. Keeping the leash in your left hand, use your right hand to give the stay signal, as you tell your dog to stay.

If your dog knows the sit/stay, then the down/stay should progress quickly, with your being able to walk around the dog within several repetitions of the command.

10. If your dog tries to get up, then say "No!" Replace him in the down position, and repeat your stay command.

11. After several repetitions you should be able to walk around your dog as he remains down. Always use successive increments between letting go of his shoulder blades and walking around him. If you approach your final goal too quickly, you will have to regress a bit in order to make your dog more reliable.

12. After each down/stay exercise go directly into the heel.

The down/stay. The leash should be put into your left hand, and your right hand should give the stay signal. You should step away from your dog on your right leg, just as in a sit/stay.

The elongated down/stay. Work around the dog in a procedure similar to that used with the sit/stay.

The down/stay. Walk completely around your dog, once he accepts your standing at his side for about a minute.

In order to retain your dog's attentiveness, try to vary the exercises. Do not always do the same thing when you stop. Sometimes do a sit/stay, sometimes a down/stay, and at other times stop, have your dog sit, and then go into the heel. The more you vary the exercises, the more interested both you and your dog will remain.

After several days of performing the down/stay, experiment to see if your dog has an understanding of the command. Give him the command and wait about five seconds before placing him down. If he goes down on command, give him exuberant praise and petting. If he looks down as you give the command, then he has an understanding of the exercise but is unwilling to give in to it. If he looks away, it means that he knows exactly what it means but feels very put out by it. These last two types of dog may have to be taught in another way to go down on command. Another behavior you may see when giving the command is simply immobility. If your dog reacts in this manner, it means that he does not comprehend the exercise. Continue to place him down with the command for a few more days.

The Down for Large Dogs

If you have difficulty trying to bring both legs of a large dog forward, then go on as follows:

1. After you have stopped and your dog is sitting on your left side in heel position, check to see which side he is leaning on. You will be able to read his position by looking at his hips. From the top (or his back) you will see less of the hip on the side he is leaning on. If you look underneath him you will see more of the leg on the side on which he is leaning. If he is sitting square—weight distributed evenly—then do the exercise as if he were leaning to his right.

Your dog should also accept being walked across while in a down/stay.

Placing a large dog into the down. Place the leash in your left hand, on the dog's shoulder blades. Lift the leg of the side he is leaning on, and press down on the shoulder blades in the same direction of the leg you have lifted.

2. Once you have ascertained the side he is leaning on, give him the down command.

3. Keep your finger pointed to the ground for about five seconds.

4. Put your leash in your left hand and put that hand on your pet's shoulder blades.

5. Begin to put downward pressure on his shoulder blades as you lift and pull forward the foreleg on the side on which he is leaning.

6. Continue the pressure until his belly or side touches the ground. As soon as he is down, give him the stay command. Continue to apply pressure on his shoulders if he appears unsettled. If he relaxes into the position, then release the pressure and begin to stand upright.

7. Gradually increase your movements around him as he remains in the down/stay.

8. Be sure to continually praise him as he listens to you.

9. After he completes this command, take him directly into a heel.

10. Try to vary the exercises so that he does not become pattern-trained. Remember that the more you vary things the more attentive your dog will be. Don't we all become lethargic when bored?

While placing a large dog into a down, put your leash in your left hand, which then goes on the shoulder blades.

Grab the leg on which he is leaning as you press down on the shoulder blades.

Reprimands

The first reprimand for the down that I will discuss is the one that will work on most dogs. The extremely stubborn ones will need the final procedure to go down on command for you. The reprimand for not going down is as follows:

1. Give your dog the command to go down, and wait about five seconds.

2. After his time is up, say "No!" in a very low growling tone.

3. Grab a hold on his lead near the snap with your strongest hand, or both hands if the dog is large.

4. Quickly bring the lead under his chin and then snap it downward very firmly. If you do this slowly, you will only choke your dog. Release quickly.

5. Your dog's response will be to go down immediately, if not sooner.

This reprimand is like shock treatment. It is done so quickly that your dog doesn't know what hit him. He will be surprised, and dogs hate surprises. After one or several of these reprimands he will go down when told.

An important facet of this procedure is the surprise. Do not repeat the reprimand or you may make your dog aggressive. If the snap did not

Down reprimand. If your dog does not go down on command after at least two weeks of repetition, grab the leash near his collar and tug down firmly, just one time, as you give a verbal reprimand. If your dog doesn't fall to the ground, place him.

The down reprimand. If the tug-down doesn't work after several days of repetition, the next step is to put your foot down. Hold the leash in your right hand, as you place your left foot where the leash and collar meet. The foot goes down quickly and firmly as you give a verbal reprimand.

get him down, then place him into the position as you did previously.

6. As soon as your dog's belly or side touches the ground, release the tight hold on your lead, and give the stay command. Always praise him enthusiastically when he behaves correctly.

For the very stubborn or dominant dog, you will need to do the following down procedure:

1. Give your dog the down command.

2. When he does not comply, say "No!" as you put all of the lead into your right hand, place your left foot on the lead near the snap, and stomp down quickly.

3. As soon as your dog is in the down position, give him the stay command, and gradually release the pressure that your foot is applying to the lead. If your pet does not try to get up, then work your way around him in small increments with each stay command.

4. If your dog gets up out of the down/stay, then use the same technique as you say "No!" Not many dogs will require more than a few of these reprimands.

Teaching your dog to do a down/stay may take up to several weeks. Do not become discouraged; persistence will be rewarded.

Preventing the Down from Becoming a "Trick"

Once he has learned it, your dog can turn the down into one of his "tricks" to try to get his way. For example, you have your dog in a sit/stay and while you are walking around him he lies down. This can either be a sign that he is tired (and you can accept it as such if you have been working him for a while) or that he is trying to "take an inch." You must make him discern the difference between the sit/stay and down/stay, or your dog will do as he pleases. If he goes down while he is supposed to be sitting, do the following:

1. Give him the heel command as you stand at his right side.

2. Take one or two steps forward.

3. As soon as your pet gets up, reiterate your sit/stay command.

This is the easiest method for getting a large dog back into a sit position when he is lying down.

If you have a small dog or puppy, you can simply lift him back into a sit. Do this procedure as follows:

1. Place one hand under his chin.

2. Lift him gently from under his chin until his front feet are underneath him. Release the pressure and pet his chest.

3. Give him the stay command.

Once your dog is doing the down/stay on command, then begin doing distraction-proofing as he works. Use the same types of distraction as when doing the sit/stay. You need to teach your dog that no matter which position he is in, he must remain attentive in all situations.

11. The Come

THIS IS THE FIRST STEP in teaching your dog to come when called. You will learn the next phase during your off-leash training. This first procedure is to ensure that your dog has a full understanding of the exercise.

Recall with a young dog. Crouching down, tell your puppy to come as you gather the leash. Praise him the entire time he comes toward you. Make him sit when he arrives in front of you.

You will be able to set and maintain certain standards while training this behavior on lead. We all want to have our dogs able to run freely and go anywhere with us. If you follow my directions one step at a time, then I will get you there.

The main criterion of the come exercise is to teach your dog to come directly to you. Your pet should make a beeline to you and sit facing you. He should remain sitting in front of you until receiving further direction. Do not accept anything less than a perfect execution of your command. You do not want your dog to be casual about coming to you. He should not sniff, take his time, or go beyond you. You should make it clear to him from the start that he is to come in quickly and directly.

You will find that this exercise may be fairly easy, compared to the last one. Everything will be very positive. You should never do anything negative to a dog who comes to you. For example, if your dog chewed the couch, do not call him to you and then punish him. He will have a bad association with the come command. You should praise your pet vigorously every time he comes to you.

Training a Puppy

When teaching the come to a puppy or to any dog that is off a lead, you must look extremely inviting. Remember that you will look most inviting when in a submissive position. With this in mind proceed as follows:

1. Begin by sitting on the floor or ground and playing with your pup. When he goes a short distance away, say his name and the "Come" command in an inviting tone as you clap your hands and open out your arms.

2. When he turns to look at you, praise him. He will want to come to you to play; so continue praising him as he comes in.

3. When he arrives in front of you, give him the "Sit" command as you place him in position.

4. Continue praising him the whole time.

5. To repeat this exercise move away from him and call him again.

Be sure not to have any distractions present when doing your initial training. When your pup is reliable on his come, then gradually increase the distractions.

If your pup does not respond to your come command at all, you should put his collar and lead on him. Break out a few treats, and reward him with the food each time he comes in. If he does not come, then bring him to you via the lead. Use constant praise the whole time he is doing the right thing.

Making the Come into a Game
You can do a fun puppy game with the help of a family member or a friend. The game is called "round robin."

Each of you positions yourself at one end of a room. You take turns calling the pup to you. Each time he comes, he is told to sit and placed in position as you give him a little treat. Before long you will find that your pup is giving a quick response to the command so that you can begin to phase out the treat. You want your pup to come because you told him to do so, not because he will receive a food reward. (A bait-trained dog can be unreliable at times.)

If you are working your pup on a lead and have already accomplished the previous exercises, then you can teach the come in a manner somewhat similar to that of teaching an older dog:

1. Place your pup in a sit or down/stay.

2. Walk around your pup a few times.

3. Stop and face your pup and give the come command. As you give the command, bend forward in order to look less dominating.

Your pup should come toward you willingly. If not, then go straight backward giving a light tug on the lead. He will get up, and as he does so praise him enthusiastically. You can stop moving backward when your pup begins coming to you.

You can also use the backward motion to correct a dog that is off course, i.e., is not coming to you but is going toward a distraction, or beyond you. Backing up will bring him back on course without having to drag him into position.

4. As your pup comes to you, gather up your leash. This will prevent him from becoming tangled up in it as he reduces the leash tension.

5. Once your pup is in front of you give him the "Sit" command.

6. If he does not sit, then place him into the position. Do not reprimand him for not following through. Your pup will eventually pick up on the pattern and sit automatically when he comes to you.

Be certain to repeat your come exercise from different directions. Call your dog as you face him, then from either side, and also from behind him. Your pet should learn to come to you from wherever you call him. You can even call him from behind some barrier so that he learns to stay and come when you are out of sight. This is a good head start on your off-lead training.

Training a Dog

The main difference between teaching a dog to come versus teaching a puppy is that you do not have to look as submissive. You can stand upright, which is the position you want to be in when calling your dog to you. If you always bend over, then your dog will pick up on that visual cue and will not come unless receiving the cue. Once a puppy has learned to come, you can reduce the submissive visual cue and go on to standing upright.

Begin your training session by doing your "warm-up" exercises, which should consist of all the exercises that you have accomplished so far.

The recall. As you say, "Come," bend over slightly and gather the leash as your dog comes to you.

The recall. Stand the full distance of the six-foot leash, facing your dog.
Do not pull on the leash as you give the command.

1. Place your dog in a stay.

2. Walk around your dog as you praise him.

3. Stop in front of your pet and face him. Be sure to stand still. You want your dog to come to you, so do not move to where he seems to be walking.

4. Give your dog the come command in an inviting tone of voice. (Be sure that you do not lose your authority in the command.)

5. As your dog comes to you, gather the leash.

The recall. Your dog should sit automatically, facing you when he reaches your position. If he does not sit automatically, give the "Sit" command. If he still doesn't sit, place him. Do not reprimand him for not sitting. This would make negative associations for the come command.

To correct a dog who doesn't come close enough for you to reach him or comes in crooked, walk backward as he nears you. This is also a good means of initially teaching the come to a young puppy.

6. If your pet does not sit automatically, then give him the "Sit" command. If he does not sit on command, then place him in the position. Always praise him whenever he performs correctly.

7. Your dog should remain in the sitting position until you give him another command. Keep in mind that if you are going to move and you wish him to remain, you should tell him to stay.

8. Always be sure to return to the heel position if you want to walk with him.

Once your dog is reliable in this exercise, you can do some distraction-proofing.

The best distraction is another dog stationed between you and your pet. Your dog must continue to come in to you straight—regardless of how much he wants to say "Hello" to the other animal.

If he tries to stop and socialize, then move backward as you give the leash a light jerk, and say "No!" As he corrects himself and comes toward you again, then praise him.

If your dog is persistently walking beyond you on the come, then you can do the following:

1. Place your dog in a stay next to a wall or other solid object.

2. Walk around him a few times; then station your back to the wall.

3. Call him to you.

Your dog will most likely come straight to you since he sees that he cannot go beyond you. If you use this procedure during a few training sessions, then you will correct the problem. This method of working your dog up against a solid bar-

If your dog tends to continue beyond you when you command him to come, place a wall or fence at your back before you call him.

rier can also be useful in teaching him to sit straight. Heel your dog around a bit; then walk against the fence or wall with him in between. When you stop, your dog will have no choice but to sit straight. If you do this persistently, then your dog will form the good habit of sitting straight.

Using the Drop-on-Recall and Down-on-the-Fly

Another aspect of the come command is one that you can use in emergency situations. This is called the "Drop-on-Recall." It will take a while to teach this procedure but it is well worth the time. An example of its usage is when your dog may be playing across the street in a residential area. You call your dog to come but suddenly see a car speeding toward him. You can either give him a visual signal or command "Down!" Your dog will drop and remain there until you give him the come command.

I will explain the procedures for teaching this behavior during off-lead training. There are, however, a few things that you can begin to practice before attaining the off-lead status.

First, teach your dog to go down on command with you standing directly in front of him.

1. Simply give him the command and a visual signal that can be seen at a distance, such as your arm raised over your head. If he does not respond to your command, back it up by either reprimanding him or placing him into position.

Signaling the down as you stand in front. A hand raised in the air is a clear signal for your dog to drop.

2. Give him the stay command as soon as he is down.

3. Very gradually increase your distance in front of him (never going farther than six feet) when doing this exercise. If at any time

Tell your dog to down as you move forward in the heel.

Your dog should drop to the ground immediately on your down command or signal.

your dog does not do as commanded, you must back up your command.

4. Once he is reliable in this exercise, begin to give him the down command as you are walking him at the heel. This is called the Down-on-the-Fly. Your dog should drop immediately when told. It may take up to a week to accomplish this.

5. When your dog is going down on the fly and you are a short distance from him, then you can begin to practice the down in conjunction with the come. Do not rush into doing this at a long distance, not yet. Your dog must first know how to come off-lead before you can introduce this difficult concept. I will expand on the procedures from this point when we discuss the off-lead come.

12. The Finish

IF YOU PLAN to teach your dog to heel off-lead, or if you intend to show your dog in an obedience trial, then you will need this exercise. The purpose of the finish is to teach your dog to go into a sit/stay at your left side in heel position from wherever he may be. For example, your dog has executed a come, and is sitting in front of you. You now want to walk with him in the heel. You can either do a finish at a standstill—which is how it is done in the obedience trial—or begin walking as you give your dog the heel command.

There are several methods of teaching this exercise. The method you use depends on which is easier for your dog. You can have him finish to your left, or go behind your back via your right side and come to a sit at your left side. This second method is easier for most dogs, so I suggest you try teaching your dog this method first. Your dog will pick up on the command quickly from the visual cues and vocal command used. Actually, he already has learned how to do this; only it will be in reverse of the normal heel. He has also learned to sit automatically when stopped at your left side, so this will also come naturally.

The finish. Place half the leash in your right hand.

The finish. Tell your dog to heel as you step back on your right leg and swing your right arm—still holding the leash—back with your leg.

Finish to the Right

1. Warm up as usual.

2. Place your dog in a sit/stay, or do a come.

3. Stand directly in front of your dog, close enough to touch his head.

4. Place half the leash in your right hand. The other half should be slack between you and your dog. If your leash is too tight, then your dog will resist performing this exercise. By this time he should be able to perform with a very loose lead regardless of any distraction.

5. At the same time that you give your dog the command "Heel!" take a big step backward with your right leg. Do not move your left leg at all— unless your dog does not pick up the cue. (I will discuss how to deal with this later.)

6. When you give the command and step back, swing your right arm backward with the same arc as your leg.

7. As your dog gets up and begins walking by your right side, bring your right leg forward (even with your left leg), simultaneously switching the leash behind your back to your left hand. If you do not step forward quickly enough, your dog will stop and sit behind you.

The finish. As you bring your right leg back even with your left, transfer the leash behind your back into your left hand. Your dog will come to your left side and sit in heel position.

When your dog sees that you are no longer heading in that backward direction, he respond by coming around to your left side and then he should sit automatically. If he does not sit, then give him the command to do so.

If your dog does not get up when you move your right leg back, do not pull him around; take a few more steps backward. When he gets up and begins to walk back, then move forward into your original position. Some dogs simply need a more visual cue for this exercise.

8. When your dog has been doing this exercise correctly for several weeks it is time to diminish the visual cues. Your objective is to be able to stand completely still and have your dog come to your left side when you tell him to heel. You will need to do this gradually. Use successive increments as you diminish the distance that you move your right leg back as you give the command. If at any time your dog does not get up as you give the command, then return to moving your leg back. With several days of practice your pet should be performing this exercise without your having to move.

If your dog is distracted when you give him the heel command, do the same reprimand as you would do if going forward. Snap and say "No!" Keep in mind, however, that you will be doing the snap with your right hand in a backward motion.

Finish to the Left

The other method of performing a finish is for your dog to come toward your left, turn around, and sit in heel position. This exercise can be more difficult for your dog than the former procedure. He may be prone to sit crookedly at your left.

There are some dogs that pick up better on this meth-od because to them it is a shortcut into heel position.

1. Place your dog either in a sit/stay or do a come.

2. Place half the lead in your left hand. The remainder of the lead—between you and your dog—should be slack.

3. As you give the heel command, step back on your left leg and swing your left arm (with the leash in it) in a backward motion.

The finish with a Halti. You should place half the leash in your right hand. As you give the heel command, step back on your right leg, and swing your right arm simultaneously backward.

4. When your dog gets up and goes back with your left leg, then bring your left leg forward as you turn your dog into the direction in which you are facing.

5. As soon as he is in the heel position, he should sit. If he does not sit automatically, then give him the sit command.

Eventually you can diminish your leg cues as your dog learns this exercise.

Training the Finish with a Halti

Everything is exactly the same as with the choke chain. Be sure not to pull as you tell your dog to heel, or you will be shutting his mouth with the pressure of the Halti. Coax him around, just as you would with the other collar. If he doesn't move, then tug and release, or take some more steps backward.

13. The Stand/Stay

Teaching your dog to stand still while being groomed and examined will be beneficial in many situations. First, your dog will be less frightened when being examined by a veterinarian, understanding what is going on as soon as he is told to stand and stay on the examining table. Second, having him stand still while being groomed and bathed will help avoid your having to take a bath with him!

Another use of this exercise is for the "Stand for Examination" in the obedience ring or for the "Stack" in a conformation trial. In all these situations your dog must not move his feet at all.

In order to help him maintain the position for a longer period, it will be helpful for you to make sure that he is standing square—equally balanced on all four legs. If he is not balanced, then he will be more likely to move. If he is being bathed or receiving a veterinary check, then this is not so bad, but if he is in the show ring it can mean a loss of many points.

The stand. Put the entire leash into your right hand, very near the clip. Your left hand gives the stand signal: an open palm moving from the dog's head toward his rear.

Most dogs will pick up on this exercise fairly quickly. There are some, however, that are very sensitive to being touched on their undersides, and they may try to move away or nip at you.

There are several different methods for getting your dog into a stand/stay. If you find that your dog gets upset with one method, try another. Just be sure that your dog does not get away with *not* doing what you command.

Stand from a Sit

1. When your dog is sitting in the heel position, place all the lead—gathered to the stitching near the clip—in your right hand.

2. Use your left hand as the visual cue for the command as follows: Spread your fingers wide; have your palm facing the dog. Begin the signal near your pet's muzzle, and sweep it toward his rear. At the same time you give this signal, also use your vocal command, "Stand."

The stand. After you give the visual and verbal command, your right hand pulls the leash forward as your left hand gently lifts your dog from the base of his ribs.

6. Put a finger or two of your right hand under his collar. Keep your left hand underneath him and rub his tummy, as you praise him.

7. After several seconds, go directly into the heel.

8. Gradually increase the amount of time that your dog remains in the stand with you rubbing his tummy.

9. As soon as he relaxes into the position (meaning he does not try to move), place the lead between your knees—your left hand should still be on his stomach—and give the stay signal with the vocal command.

3. As soon as your visual cue is complete, gently pull forward (not upward) on the lead with your right hand. Place your left hand on the dog's abdomen just under his rib cage (the area of the solar plexus).

4. Lift upward on his underside as you pull forward on the lead.

5. As soon as he is in the stand position, release the pull on the lead as well as the pressure on his abdomen.

The stand. As your dog remains standing, you should rub his tummy. This stabilizes the dog, making him more likely to remain in one spot.

The stand/stay. When your dog is steady, place the leash between your knees, while keeping your left hand under your dog. Give the stay signal with the right hand as you give the verbal command, "Stay!"

will be able to make a complete circle around him. And once you can do circles, then you can let up on your collar hold and begin walking around without touching him, gradually increasing your distance.

If your dog tries to move at any time throughout this exercise, use your vocal reprimand only. Then replace his feet in their original position and give your "Stay!" command.

Once your dog can perform this exercise reliably in a quiet situation, you can gradually increase his exposure to distractions. Doing a stand/stay with distractions may be difficult because your dog is in a position of action. Be persistent and you will succeed.

10. As soon as the signal is complete, return your right hand to your dog's collar, with the leash in it. Continue rubbing your pet, moving your hand around to his side and up to his back. Gradually increase the areas you touch as he remains in the stand/stay.

When you are able to rub your pet all over, it is time to start moving yourself around him in stages while he remains in position. You should gradually advance in successive increments beginning with your movement around his hind end and then up and back along his sides. Eventually you

The stand/stay. As your dog remains in the stay, begin to move around his back end first, while continually touching him.

Throughout this training be sure to vary the sequence and kinds of exercise. You do not want your dog to become pattern-trained. You can do a stand/stay after doing a finish, or just after stopping. You can also do it from a stay or after a come. If you keep your dog guessing, he will be more attentive.

Stand from a Heel

Another way of performing this exercise is from the heel. If you are planning on showing your dog in a conformation trial, then this is the way you should teach him to "Stack." Or, if your dog is sensitive to being lifted into position, you can be more successful using this method. Another reason to use this method is if your dog is a Great Dane and far outweighs you.

1. Walk your dog at the heel.

2. Before stopping, take all the leash into your right hand.

3. As you stop, give your dog the visual signal with your left hand and say his name and the command "Stand!"

"Stand for Examination." While your dog remains in the stand/stay, he can receive a full examination from his teeth, to . . .

. . . his ears, to . . .

. . . his entire body.

The stand/stay makes it easier to locate injuries or parasites.

The stand/stay. As you maintain pressure under the dog's hind leg, put the leash between your legs, and use your right hand to give the dog the stay signal, along with your vocal command.

The stand/stay. Begin by continually touching your dog as you walk around him, back end first.

4. Place your left hand on the stifle (or knee) of his left hind leg.

5. Grab his collar with your right hand.

6. Follow the same procedures I described previously for gradually increasing the examination and your motion around your pet.

7. When you are finished with the stand/stay, go directly into the heel again.

Once your dog has a full understanding of this exercise, you can mix up the commands. For example, do a stand/stay and then a sit/stay. Or do a sit/stay, come, finish, and then a stand/stay. I do recommend, however, that you do not do a come from a stand/stay. Your dog may have a tendency to move in anticipation of the come command.

Completion of On-Lead Obedience Training

Congratulations! Upon accomplishing this exercise you have completed on-leash basic obedience. Your dog should be listening on only one command regardless of the situation. He should be disciplined and attentive to your every movement. He will have an understanding of his environment and where his place is in it.

14. Behavior Modification

THERE ARE SOME dogs that may have persistent behavior problems even though they do well with their on-lead obedience.

Jumping Up

When dogs greet each other they touch noses and sniff each other's odors. As humans we simply say hello or shake hands. When your dog greets you he is just trying to do the same in his language. Since most people tower above their dog, the animal feels that he must jump up to reach the person's muzzle. Other animals simply push their noses between your legs, so that they can identify your scent. To a dog these behaviors are instinctive. To us they are abhorrent. To stop this behavior you will either have to change your dog's instinct or make yourself available to this greeting. Let's first discuss how to communicate your greeting in canine language.

To make yourself available for the canine greeting you must crouch down to your dog's level and be prepared for much licking and nose pushing in your face. You may also be bowled over if you have a large dog. While this may not bother some people, it may be quite uncomfortable for others. Personally, I do not appreciate being slimed.

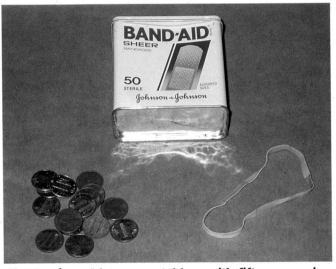

The "no-jump" box: a metal box with fifteen pennies. Use the elastic to keep the box closed.

I recommend this crouched greeting for a young puppy or small dog, but not for an older, large dog. This greeting also helps with those dogs that are submissive wetters. You look less threatening when you are crouched down.

If you want to prevent this from becoming a behavior problem, teach your dog to sit for attention. When you greet him, tell him to sit. If he does not, put him into the sit position, and then praise him. If you do this consistently, he will learn to sit when he says "Hello."

The "No-Jump" Box

If you wish to remain standing upon entering your house or dog pen, then do the following:

1. Make a "no-jump" box. This can be a metal Band-Aid box or small tin can with fifteen or so pennies in it. Make sure the cover is secure.

2. When your dog goes to jump up, shake the can hard in an up-and-down motion, just once or twice, as you say "No!"

3. When he crouches down and stops trying to jump up, praise and pet him.

For dogs that are insensitive to this aural reprimand—or if you simply do not have your penny can with you—then you must either push off or knock down your dog as he jumps up. Do this with your knee in his chest on his way up or with your hand if he is already on you. Always say "No!" when pushing him off.

You must be consistent with this correction. If there are any family members who either invite or allow your dog to jump up, then it will take a long time for him to understand that he must not behave in this manner.

Preventing and Setting "Traps" to Stop Bad Behavior

One of the many bad habits that your dog may develop is jumping on your furniture. You can avoid this by training him as a pup, or, if you already allowed him on the furniture and have decided that you want him off, then you can correct it.

First, let's discuss how to prevent the problem. Simply do not bring your pup onto any furniture—not the couch, the bed, or any chair that you have not allotted to him. If he tries to get up, then push him down firmly as you say "No!" Once he is remaining down and looking at you, praise him.

If you already have the problem, then you will have to consistently push or pull him off as you say "No!" Some dogs will become wise to the fact that they can't get on the sofa when you are around, but will do so when you are out. In this case you will need to either turn up the cushions, or set up a "trap." The trap should consist of aluminum pots and pans tied to the couch cushions with fishing line. Place the pots precariously on the edge of the back of the couch. Tie the fishing line to the front of the cushions. When your dog jumps up, he will be surprised by the noise and action of the pots. If you set up this "trap" daily, then you will cure this behavior within a short time.

This trap can also be set up for a dog that gets into the garbage. Place the garbage can next to your counter edge. Place the pots precariously on the edge of the counter. Tie or tape the fishing line to the far side of the garbage can and to some inviting items inside the can. When your dog tries his normal routine, he will receive a surprise. He will be cured of this behavior after several incidents.

Dealing Directly with an Incident

Another way to teach your dog to stay out of the garbage is to do as follows (although this may be difficult with a large dog):

1. Grab your dog by the scruff of the neck—and collar, if your dog is large. (Be sure not to call him to you and then do it. Never associate the come with anything negative.)

2. Drag your dog to the garbage mess.

3. Shove his nose next to it.

4. Shake him once or twice as you say "No!"

5. Put him in a small, dark place and isolate him there for at least a half hour. If the behavior occurs again, increase his isolation time in ten-minute increments.

6. Upon letting your dog out of isolation do not pet or communicate with him in any manner for another half hour. Your dog will come out of isolation looking very droopy.

Commercial Aids

There are also several products on the market that can aid in training your dog to stay out of the garbage and off the furniture. One is called a Scat Mat. It comes in varying sizes: long and narrow for a couch or semicircular for garbage cans and plants. It works by either emitting a high-frequency tone or electric stimulation when it is touched.

Another product is the Snappy Trainer. It's a variation on the mousetrap, but makes more noise when it closes. It can be placed strategically in the areas you wish to teach your dog not to go upon.

If you are firm and consistent, then you will cure the bad behavior. If you are inconsistent, then the problem will intensify. Keep in mind that dogs do not have the same reasoning capabilities as humans. From the dog's viewpoint, he can either do something or not do it. He does not understand the "sometimes," "maybes," and other variations. If you present everything in a cut-and-dried manner, then he will learn faster.

Mouthing

There are several situations in which mouthing (and sometimes biting) occurs. Your dog may be playing with you, as he would with another dog, or he may be asserting his dominance or simply being over-protective of a toy or other object. Let's take these situations one at a time.

Prevention

First of all, you can prevent this bad behavior from occurring if you teach your dog as a pup that he cannot put his mouth on you or anyone else. In order to do this, proceed as follows:

1. When your pup puts his mouth on you, grab him by the scruff of his neck, look him in the eye, and say "No!" in a low, growling tone.

2. Hold him in position until he looks away and/or blinks his eyes.

3. Let go slowly. If he proceeds to bite on you as you let go, snatch his scruff again.

4. You should be able to let go slowly without your pup going after your hand again.

5. If the alpha shake does not work, then do the alpha rollover. In this situation throw your pup onto his back as you pin him down by the scruff of his neck. Placing a hand on either side of his neck will facilitate this action.

6. If he struggles as you let up on him, pin him again.

You will have to be very persistent with this if your dog has gotten away with this behavior for a while. He may try to move out from under you, or squeal. Do not give in. Always maintain your scruff hold until he shows signs of submission.

If your pup is very young, an alpha shake should be sufficient. Remember, do not to give in, no matter how pitiful he looks.

When you successfully accomplish this reprimand and your dog is sitting looking at you, give him one of his toys and praise him as he plays with it.

Stopping the Behavior

If you have a dog that has been doing this mouthing for a long time and you have finally decided that you've had enough, be sure to first try the alpha shake and rollover before doing the next exercise. If you hesitate or give in too soon, you may have to use a more formidable method.

This next reprimand is for the dog that is biting on your hand or leg as you walk him. You can also use this reprimand on a very aggressive dog. It keeps you safe from gnashing teeth, as well as calms your dog immediately. I call this next reprimand the "Hang Up."

1. Begin by making sure that your dog has a collar and lead on.

2. When your dog tries to mouth, nip, or show any type of aggression, place the lead in either your strongest hand or both hands.

3. Pull upward quickly as you say "No!"

4. Your dog's front feet should be off the ground. Be sure not to lift him entirely off the ground; you do not want to snap his neck.

5. Hold him up until he goes limp, or until about ten seconds have passed.

6. When you let him down, give him a command, such as heel or sit/stay.

Repeat this procedure as necessary.

This exercise may be difficult if you are a little person with a big dog. For this to work, you will have to be able to tough it out.

Dealing with Overpossessiveness

Many dogs are overpossessive. They either grew up with a pack of dogs, or simply weren't taught about dropping an object on command. This can pop up around mealtime, or simply when playing around. It can be very dangerous behavior if you have children.

You can prevent this aggression from occurring if you teach your pet as a pup that nothing bad happens when you take food from him or pick up a toy he is chewing on. Practice intervening in these ways over a peroid of time and always be sure to give back or replace the removed item in some way.

Never try to pull an object out of your dog's mouth. This will only cause him to pull back more aggressively. The best approach is to teach your dog to "Drop" an object on command.

1. Place one hand under his lower jaw as you give the command "Drop." If he does not comply, place your other hand over the top of his muzzle.

2. Squeeze his lips into his teeth, as you say "No!" Your dog will drop the object because he will not like biting on his own lips.

3. As soon as the object drops into your hand, praise your pet and give it back to him.

4. Repeat this exercise often, until your dog will drop a toy or piece of food on your command.

Excessive Barking

There are several methods that you can use to cure the excessive barker. You will first have to analyze the situations in which this behavior occurs in order to solve the problem.

Many dogs will bark from fear. This is the most difficult type of excessive barking to cure. You cannot approach a fearful dog in any aggressive manner or the bark may turn into a bite.

You can recognize a fear barker in the following ways:

• As he barks he is backing away.

• His tail is down low.

• His hackles (fur along the spine) are raised.

• His head will be held low, with his ears laid back.

There are several ways to cure this problem. First, do consistent obedience training. Second, let your dog greet the person he is barking at by having the person crouch down with his side facing your dog. The person should avoid eye contact with the dog and keep his hands tucked into his stomach, not stretched out toward the dog. Heel your dog around the person and do several sit/stays on the way. When your dog is no longer paying attention to the person, tell your dog "Break." Let him go up and sniff the person. Be sure to keep your lead loose, so that you do not show any anxiety about the situation. Have the person give your dog treats. This will ensure a pleasant association with your pet.

Excessive territorial barking can be annoying to dog owners and their neighbors.

You can ascertain that he is barking at an intruder by his body language and the tone used in the bark:

• Your dog will be trying to look as big as he can.

• The fur along his spine will be raised.

• His ears will be forward.

• His tail will be straight out or raised over his back.

• His tone will be loud, fast, and deep.

Inside and Outside Territorial Barking

There are two main situations in which this problem of territorial barking occurs: inside your house or vehicle and outside in the yard. The problem is considerably more difficult to cure when your dog's behavior takes place outside or when you are away from home, but it can be done.

I will first address correction in the enclosed area. Your dog will not be able to avoid the correction as long as you have a collar and lead on him.

1. You must have a command, such as "Enough," or "Stop." When your dog is barking excessively, use this command.

2. If he does not listen, then grab his muzzle in one hand, bring your face close to him, and look him in the eye.

3. Shake his head from side to side as you say "No Bark," or just "No!"

4. Let go of his muzzle and wait to see if he tries again. If so, repeat the reprimand. If he is quiet, praise him.

Many dogs become wise to the fact that they will be reprimanded for barking and will dodge your efforts at grabbing the muzzle. If this happens, then use the correction for the outside dog as follows:

When reprimanding your dog for excessive barking, place one hand around his muzzle as you stare him in the eye and say, "No Bark!" in a low reprimand tone. Don't let go until your dog blinks and looks away from you.

can use the same reprimands as are successful in the dealing with the problem of the territorial barker.

Sometimes lonely dogs will bark excessively. A dog that has been left behind for a long period with no other company may start to howl. Howling is the canine way of rounding up others. Curing this problem requires cunning and deception.

If you can manage several days at home, this will ensure the greatest success.

1. Leave your house just as you normally do, putting things away, picking up your car keys, etc.

1. Grab the lead that is dragging alongside your dog.

2. Bring your dog to you. Do not say "Come."

3. Grab his muzzle when he is next to you and execute the reprimand. Repeat as necessary.

Another means of solving the problem is to shake your penny can in your dog's face as you say "No!" This method is very easy, but you must have your penny can handy at all times.

Barking for Attention or from Being Left Alone

Some dogs will bark because they want your attention. This is a learned response. Your pet must have done it at one time and liked the results, so he continues whenever he wants you to play with him. You

2. If your dog begins barking as you leave, go back inside and shake the penny can in his face or do the muzzle shake, as you say "No!"

3. Repeat as often as necessary.

4. Soon your dog will begin to wait a little longer before beginning his noise.

5. Remain close by and look in a window if you can. As soon as he begins barking again, go inside and reprimand him again.

6. If your dog begins to be quiet for a longer period of time, return to your house and give him a treat and praise him.

7. Gradually increase the time that he is alone before you return to him.

Commercial Aids

If all else fails, you will have to purchase a Barker Breaker or Bark Inhibitor collar. The first emits a high-frequency beep when the dog barks, and the second can be set on different levels of electrical stimulation to zap him when he barks. If you want your dog to bark for protection, but not to be excessive about it, there is the Bark Diminisher collar. This collar allows three barks, and, if the barking continues, then gives a zap.

Chewing

Dogs have a need to chew. It is their way of passing the time and relieving anxiety. They cannot read books and very rarely pay attention to the shows on television, so they need another pastime. Your dog should always have plenty of toys available (at least three), and the toys should be rotated every day or two. This ensures that your pet will remain content.

Prevention

It is easier to do preventive training on this problem than corrective training. From the beginning never let your pup have anything other than dog toys. Do not be tempted to give him an old shoe or towel. If you make this error, then be prepared to have your newer shoes or bathroom towels ripped to shreds.

Any time your pup puts his mouth on anything other than his toys, reprimand him immediately.

1. Grab him by the scruff of his neck.

2. Shake him and say "No!"

3. Fling him away from the object he was chewing.

4. Give him one of his toys. When he begins to play with it, praise him.

Pups go through several teething stages. The first occurs between three and three and a half months. They lose their front baby teeth as their adult incisors come in. You may see your pup chewing and pulling with his front teeth. Just when you think it is over, the back teeth begin to come in. This happens when your pup is about five months, and lasts for four months. It is at this time that the most

chewing problems occur. If you are very consistent with the preventive measures, then this stage will pass uneventfully. If, however, you let your pup chew on household objects because you thought it was "cute," you will have a problem chewer.

Corrective Training

Most problem chewers will do their damage when you are not with them. They have learned that they will be reprimanded if they chew the couch in front of you, but that they can get away with it if you aren't around. Keep in mind that dogs do have good memories. How else could they remember their training, or a place that they have not been to in a long time?

The first method of teaching your dog to not chew is to put him in his crate whenever you go anywhere. Although this does not address the problem directly, it keeps your house in one piece.

The second method is similar to the reprimand I discussed in the chapter on housebreaking.

1. Grab your dog by the scruff (and collar, if your dog is large).

2. Drag him to the chewed object.

3. Put his nose down next to the object.

4. Shake his neck once or twice as you say "No!"

5. Place him in isolation for a half hour. Gradually increase the isolation time by ten minutes with every bad incident.

If your dog barks or scratches at the door, open the door, lunge inside as you say "No!" and slam the door. You may have to do this several times during your pet's initial isolation session. Another method you can use is to shake the can when you open the door.

Some dogs do not chew the object they steal, but parade it in front of their owners. They know that the person's reaction will be to try to take it from his mouth. Your dog has learned that this can be a fun game. After all, who never played tag as a child? It is a great way for your dog to get your attention and to exercise at the same time.

For dogs that enjoy this game, your best bet is to keep their collar and lead on at all times. As soon as he appears with the kitchen towel or stuffed animal, do the following:

1. Tell your dog to "Drop."

2. If he does not comply, grab his lead, bring him to you, and push his upper lips into his teeth.

3. He will drop the object. When he does so, praise him, and give him one of his own toys.

Never oblige your dog by chasing him. This will only increase his enjoyment in the game.

Digging

Digging is the most difficult behavior problem to solve. A dog has the instinct to dig. He will dig if he is left outside, to relieve his boredom, or if he is either very cold or hot. A hole has great insulation against the elements. A dog will also dig when he has the scent of another animal, such as a mole or groundhog. Before you know it you have a "lunar landscape" instead of flower beds. Once again, you can stop this behavior right away, if you begin with your dog as a pup.

1. If you catch your pup digging, say "No!" and push him away.

2. Occupy him with something positive, such as one of his toys or some obedience work.

Another method of teaching your dog not to dig is to place a mousetrap or Snappy Trainer in the hole and cover it with a bit of dirt. When your dog goes to dig at the hole he will receive a surprise. The mousetrap should not hurt him, but the snapping sound will startle him.

The best prevention for the problem digger is to never leave him outside unattended. Any dog that is left outside by himself for a long period will dig— out of boredom.

When All Else Fails

If you find that you are unable to implement these behavior modifications, you may want to consult a professional dog trainer. You do not want to cause your dog to become aggressive out of frustration or misunderstanding.

15. Introduction to Off-Lead

THE GOAL OF EVERY TRAINER is to have his or her dog listen as well without a lead as with one. This allows more freedom, both for you and your dog. You will be able to go anywhere and trust that your pet will listen. There have been many instances in which I have taken my dogs to shopping malls to perform training demonstrations. My dogs are completely relaxed and attentive to every move I make. I never at any time have to put a training collar or lead on them.

Another situation in which the off-lead training has proved helpful is during travel. Rest stops tend to be chaotic and full of distractions. A dog that is attentive off-lead will make it a lot easier on his owner. You would be able to take him to a grassy area, release him, let him relieve himself, and then heel him back to your vehicle—all without a leash.

The off-lead training has proved most fruitful whenever I use my animals in a production. We have worked through the filming of television commercials, advertisements, and films. To my dogs it seemed to be just another chance to perform, and they always appear to enjoy showing off. Sometimes I would have to stand more than thirty feet away and use only a visual cue to instruct one of my dogs. With an animal that is completely distraction-proofed and off-lead-trained, the task is easy.

Making the Transition to Off-Lead

Throughout this book I have been describing training procedures that would allow a quick switch-over into off-lead work. If you use a loose lead at all times, are consistent with distinctive vocal tones, and follow through with all commands, then you will ensure a smooth transition.

Before undertaking this advanced training your dog should be 95-percent reliable working on a lead.

Your dog is ready for advanced training when he:

- Heels without pulling

- Is able to remain in a stay for several minutes

- Comes without hesitation

- And listens on one command, regardless of any distractions around him.

This may take two to four weeks from the start of your teaching the stand/stay. The amount of time it takes depends on how often you work with your dog, your consistency, and how extensively he is distraction-proofed. Do not rush into advanced training. If you are methodical and repetitive in working with your dog, he will be reliable.

Gradualism

I have mentioned successive increments in many previous exercises. For advanced training this especially becomes the key phrase. You must proceed in successive increments so that your performance criteria gradually become higher, matching the rise in your expectations of your dog's capabilities. Do not jump from one level to another before the previous level has been successfully attained and maintained.

The careful timing of your vocal tones and visual cues is essential when teaching your dog to listen without a lead. If your timing is off even the slightest bit, you wind up spending the bulk of your training session chasing your dog. One of the ways you can test to see if your dog is ready is to use your "No!" reprimand before snapping with your lead. If your pet responds to the vocal reprimand, that is a sure sign that he understands how to correct himself and remain attentive.

Preparation for Off-Lead Work

To prepare your dog for responding to you solely on a verbal and visual level, proceed as follows:

1. Instead of gathering your lead before stopping, simply stop. If your dog sits as he halts beside you, praise him. If he continues walking, say "No," and make him do a finish to correct his position. For the inattentive dog it may help to say "No!" as you stop. This will teach him to think about what happens in this situation. After several training sessions, you should not have to reprimand your dog as you stop. Any time your dog stops out of heel position, correct him by making him finish.

2. While heeling, do a lot of turns. The sharper the turns, the better you will be able to make your point. You must decrease your leash snapping and use your body language to correct your dog. A turn accomplishes this goal.

3. When you tell your dog to come, you should not pull him to you or pull up on the lead when he arrives. The leash should remain loose at all times. If your dog begins to veer away from his direct path to you, then go backward and lean forward. This will encourage him to come in straighter.

Your dog will not actually be off-lead for several weeks. He will first learn to respond to you from a distance, with his stays and comes. He will also learn to remain at your side without a direct connection between you. Much of the off-lead training involves "faking out" your dog. He will think he is on the lead when he actually isn't. He must learn that you can control him from any distance and even when you are out of sight.

Gather the long lead by extending your arms to their fullest, grabbing the slack to make a loop, then repeating these motions until it is all gathered.

Equipment

Your main piece of equipment is a 15- or 20-foot canvas lead. This will allow you to gradually increase your distance from your dog, and will also enable you to catch him if the need arises. This lead is not meant for jerking your dog's collar. It is not as comfortable for your hand as your leather training lead.

Begin the lesson by using your six-foot lead so you can warm up your pet without hurting your hand. Once he is being attentive you can switch over to the long lead.

Many people dislike this long lead because it is difficult to manipulate. It has a tendency to collect knots, get mixed up in your pet's legs, and be stepped on. Don't worry. If you persevere you will not need it for long!

It will be helpful to devise a way to gather your lead to avoid entanglement. I have found that the most efficient means is to stretch it to the width of my outstretched arms, bring one hand to the other, and gather, repeating until the lead is entirely gathered. This action is similar to looping a rope or hose.

It would be wise to practice gathering your lead before you try using it with your dog. You will find that he will come to you quite fast from what seems to be some distance, so that the actual time you have to gather your leash will be very short. If you are flittering with your lead as your pet comes toward you, he will not come in straight and may even go beyond you. Gather the lead methodically and quickly in order to guide your dog correctly.

The other equipment you will need is a piece of cotton clothesline. This type of rope is soft, lightweight, and strong. The piece should be two to three feet long. You will need to buy more than you need initially so that you can replace it down the road. Your dog will have this attached to his collar for several months as your way of reinforcing a command if required.

To install this rope on the collar, first fold it in half and put a knot on the bottom and in the middle. Put the loop end through the moving ring of the choke chain, thread the rope through the loop, and pull tight.

You are to have your dog wear this rope from Phase Three of off-lead training, through the initial three months that you are working him off-lead.

16. Off-Lead Training

Off-lead training progresses through several stages to achieve the desired results. You have take it one phase at a time.

The first procedure involves increasing the distance during the stay exercises while walking around your dog as he first sits and then is in the down.

1. Place your dog in the sit/stay or down/stay.

2. As you walk around your dog, slowly let the lead play out. You will be spiraling outward from you dog.

Off-lead Phase 1, sit/stay. As your dog remains sitting, you gradually increase your distance as you circle around him.

Phase 1

You should practice Phase 1 for a week before going to Phase 2. This first phase concentrates on doing long-distance stays and comes. These two procedures tend to be the most important for the average pet owner. If you are planning to show your dog in obedience trials, then you will also have to put equal time into working on leash-reduction techniques as you go through Phase 1 off-lead.

Off-lead Phase 1, down/stay. As your dog remains down, you gradually increase your distance as you circle around him.

3. Praise your pet occasionally as he remains in position.

4. If he gets up, say "No!" immediately. If he does not reseat or go back down, run directly to him, grab the lead next to his collar and give him the appropriate physical reprimand: an upward jerk for the sit or a downward jerk for the down. If he begins to run away from you, then gather your lead and bring him back to where you told him to stay.

5. Once your dog has been replaced, walk around him gradually increasing your distance.

6. The next time you do a stay, continue to increase your distance.

At this point you should only go the distance of your leash. You should also work on anti-anticipation techniques. Many dogs have learned that when their handler stops and looks at them the next command will be to come. To avoid this, the second procedure involves working on the stay while stoppping every so often, but *not* calling your dog to come. If he anticipates, reprimand him accordingly; if he remains in his stay, praise him.

Practice your come command from any position around your dog. Begin by increasing the distance of the come gradually. The first come should be from 10 feet, the second from 15, and if you have a 20-foot lead, then do your final distance at the full length. Any time your dog strays from his direct beeline to you, say "No!" go backward, and continue reeling in the leash. When your dog corrects himself and returns to his direct approach, praise him all the way. You are essentially guiding him with

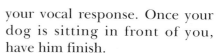

Off-lead Phase 1. Walking around the dog as he stays, gradually letting out the leash.

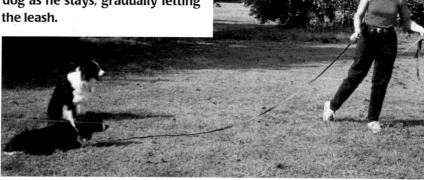

Off-lead Phase 1, with dog distraction.

your vocal response. Once your dog is sitting in front of you, have him finish.

As your dog gets used to the long-distance stays and comes, begin hiding behind objects such as vehicles, trees, and bushes. Do not, however, drop your lead at any time; you will only be challenging the extent of your dog's reliability.

During Phase 1 off-lead training you should continue to build on the time that your dog remains in the stay. He can remain in a sit/stay comfortably for up to three minutes (unless it is a very hot day) and a down/stay indefinitely. (You can not expect this, however, without having worked up to it first.)

A good place to practice this first phase of off-lead is a park or a shopping center sidewalk, where there are vehicles, people, and other animals. Working your dog while at the veterinarian's office is also an excellent opportunity to distraction-proof. You must teach your dog to behave at all times, even when under stress.

Off-lead Phase 2. Gradually increase the distance as you walk around your dog.

1. Warm up your dog with some obedience exercises he is familiar with.

2. When you have your dog stay, whether it is a sit or a down, go out to the end of your long leash and begin walking around him.

Off-lead Phase 2. You drop the long leash as you continue walking around your dog.

Phase 2

After having worked four to seven days with Phase 1 off-lead work, you should be ready for Phase 2. Up to this point you have always had a lead in your hand. Your dog knows that he must respond properly, not only because of your vocal and visual cues, but also because you can back yourself up with a physical reprimand. In this phase of training you will be "faking him out" by dropping the lead as he remains in a stay. Your dog will gradually understand that you no longer have the lead in your hand, but he will be conditioned enough by then so that it won't matter.

3. While you are walking, drop the leash nonchalantly behind your back. Do not place it on the ground, for your dog will realize quickly that he is unattached.

4. Once you drop the lead, continue walking around your dog in both directions.

5. Be sure to remain within about a 15 or 20-foot radius.

6. On returning to the end of your lead, step on it with one or both feet.

7. Give your dog the "Come" command.

When preparing to call your dog during Off-lead Phase 2, step on your leash.

If your pet comes straight to you, praise him the whole way. If he veers away from his direct path, grab the lead and pull firmly as you take a few steps backward. Be certain to use your "No!" with the leash jerk. As soon as your dog corrects his path, return to praising him. If he tries to go beyond you, grab his lead next to the collar and go backward a few steps as you guide him in front of you. If he is moving away from you quickly, then step on the lead, say "No!" and gather the lead as he comes in to you.

8. When your dog is sitting in front of you, gather up your lead. Do not walk away from him to do this.

9. Once your lead is gathered, do a finish.

During Phase 2 off-lead you begin working with letting out the lead as you heel your dog:

1. First, make sure that your dog is heeling correctly for several minutes.

2. When your dog is attentive, begin to let the leash out as you walk. Be sure to do a lot of turns and stops to maintain your dog's attention. The lead should eventually be dragging about eight feet behind your dog as you walk.

3. Should your dog begin to heel wide, do a left turn into him. If he is at your side but not keeping his eyes on you, do a right turn.

Off-lead Phase 2, heeling. The leash is let out, dragging behind your dog's hind legs. You maintain a hold on the leash from behind your back with your right hand.

Proper attachment of pull tab.

4. If your dog is very distracted and not staying with you at all, grab the lead next to his collar and jerk as you say "No!"

Continue to work on these exercises in distraction situations. A public park is the best place to practice. Not only does it give you a large open area, but it provides many distractions.

Phase 3

This phase is essentially an elongation of the procedures used in Phase 2. In successive increments, you expand the radius of your circles and begin calling your dog away from the leash.

It would be helpful if you could enlist the aid of a friend during these procedures. Having someone else to step on the lead will give you more confidence in the situation. Remember that your dog can sense your moods, so you want him to smell leadership and authority, not nervousness. It would also be helpful to find another person to assist you during your drop-on-recall exercise. I will explain how to do this a little later.

Be sure that your training area has any number of things that you can hide behind. If throughout Phases 1 and 2 you have been going out of sight, then that should not pose any problems at this point.

1. Before you begin warming up, put the pull tab on your dog's collar. From now on, whenever you need to do a leash reprimand you will do it with the pull tab.

2. Begin by doing some heel work with your lead dragging eight feet behind your dog.

3. Stop and do a sit/stay. Walk around your dog and drop your lead as you did in Phase 2.

4. Gradually increase the radius of the circles around your pet.

5. When doing a come command, return to your lead but do not step on it. Do the come.

Off-lead Phase 3, recall. You leave the leash on the ground as you perform the exercise with a dog distraction.

6. The next time you do this procedure, stand two to four feet away from the lead.

7. Gradually increase your distance and change your angle away from the lead. This is to teach your dog to come to you instead of following the path of the lead.

If your dog is coming in without hesitation, then you will no longer need to stretch out your lead before dropping it. You can drop the lead next to your dog before you leave his side.

If you have a small dog, be sure that your long lead is very lightweight. Many dogs will slow down when they feel the drag of the lead behind them as they walk. It's best to make sure before you start that the lead is not heavy.

When your dog is coming directly to you from a distance of over 40 feet, you can begin to hide behind objects on his stay and call him to you while you are out of sight. When you call him, make sure that there are not any objects in his path that can entangle his long lead.

Off-lead Phase 3, down/stay with a Halti. The leash is actually attached to the dog's regular collar and laid down beside the dog.

Off-lead Phase 3, stand/stay. The dog remains in one place with the long leash laid down at his side.

8. The whole time your dog is coming to you, praise him. If he veers in the wrong direction, say "No!" When he returns to the proper course, praise him.

9. After your dog has come and is sitting facing you, do the finish. Do not, however, pick up his lead before doing so. By this time he should finish without leash guidance. If your dog does not follow through readily, then you will have to grab the pull tab and snap with a "No!" Be sure to practice more on this exercise if your dog will not perform it without being pulled.

Off-lead Phase 3, recall. The dog is performing a recall from a distance of more than 50 feet. The farther away the dog is from you, the faster he will come when you call him.

Off-Lead Heel

The most difficult behavior to teach off-lead is the heel. You must prepare your dog by doing a lot of erratic turns, changing pace and stopping often. Any time your dog continues after you have stopped, make him do a finish. Sometimes it is helpful to turn just before stopping.

1. When you start doing the heel, begin with the lead in your hand.

Off-lead Phase 3, heeling. The leash is allowed to completely drag as your dog walks with you.

2. Gradually let it out as you walk. If your dog is being attentive you can drop the lead entirely and let it drag behind.

3. Any time your dog tries to get ahead, step on the lead, say "No!" and do a turn, coaxing your dog back to your side by slapping your left leg.

Try to use vocals and visuals before snapping on the pull tab. Do not, however, let your dog get out of reach. If your dog realizes that you cannot control him, then he will never listen without a lead. Take your time, go step by step, and be quick. If you are consistent with your timing, then it will be smooth sailing.

Phase 4

Your actual off-lead work begins in this phase. Your dog must be working well on Phase 3 with distractions, or you should not attempt these exercises. Do not think that your dog can perform everything without a lead that he can with a dragging lead. This must be built up. As with all training procedures, these exercises must be attempted in small increments or you will overwhelm your dog and lose some of his reliability. If this were to happen, you would have to regress to attain your dog's respect for your commands.

1. Begin this lesson by working for ten minutes on your Phase 3 exercises.

2. When you place your dog in a sit/stay, unclip the long line and let it drop next to him.

3. Walk around your dog in a six-foot-diameter circle.

4. Do a come in front of your dog. Be sure to praise him when he responds properly.

5. Make him do a finish.

6. Before beginning to heel, take the pull tab in your left hand.

7. While your dog is walking next to you, drop the tab.

8. Any time your dog gets more than six inches from your left side, reach for the pull tab, snap, and say "No!" When he is back in position, praise him.

9. The next time you stop, do a down/stay. Once again, walk around in a six-foot radius, and call your dog while facing him.

Hold the pull tab as you begin heeling.

You should not work off the lead for much more than ten minutes on the first try. After this time is up, return to the Phase 3 exercises for a while, and then end the session. Each time you train your dog, gradually increase the amount of time you work without the lead. Within several weeks your dog should be working off-lead throughout the training session. Even though your dog may be doing this, keep the pull tab attached to his collar for extra insurance. It doesn't hurt to be careful, especially if your dog happens to be easily distracted at any time.

The following come should be done from his side—and eventually do some from behind him. When your dog will come to you from any position at a distance of six feet, begin gradually to increase your distance on the stays and comes.

If your dog fails to come at any time, then reprimand him as follows:

1. Grab your dog's pull tab.

2. Back up a few steps as you say come; jerk him toward you as you step back.

3. Always make him sit when he reaches you.

4. Repeat three times or until you are in the place you called him from.

These jerks should be very firm. But be sure to praise your dog when he is sitting facing you.

The Come, Off-Lead from a Break

The most important exercise to practice is having your dog come to you while he is on his break. This should first be practiced while you still are holding your long lead, so you can back up your command if needed. When your dog is reliable you can drop the lead and do the come from a distance. Eventually you will be able to have your dog come to you when you are out of sight.

Off-Lead Training with a Halti

The training phases are similar to those with the choke chain. In Phase 1 you elongate the stays and comes, with the leash attached to the Halti. Phase 2 is where you begin to wean your dog off the head collar.

The only difference between your normal Phase 2 dropping of the leash during the stays and comes is that you are to attach your 20-foot lead to your dog's regular flat buckle or snap-on collar before you tell him to stay. Still wearing the Halti, your dog doesn't acknowledge the change.

When you complete a recall, change the leash back to the Halti before you do a finish.

Upon entering Phase 3 off-lead training, place your pull tab on the ring of the Halti where you would normally attach your leash. Place the 20-foot lead on the flat collar. If your dog tries to leave your side during the heel exercise (as the long leash is dragging), grab the pull tab to correct him. If he breaks a stay or doesn't come in straight, first grab the long leash, and then do your close-up correction with the pull tab.

For Phase 4 training, begin with the pull tab attached to the Halti. This will be your sole means of physical correction, so you will need to be quick. Do not let your dog stray a single inch from your side as you heel! If he does, correct him by grabbing the pull tab and jerking him back into position as you say "No!"

When your pet is reliable on the initial Phase 4 training—i.e., able to perform all exercises with-

Off-lead Phase 4, heeling with a Halti.

Off-lead Phase 4, sit/stay with a Halti. Phantom is in a sit/stay, as he is waiting for the come command.

out correction—it is time to put the pull tab on the regular flat collar. Within several months you will be able to reduce the amount of training sessions in which you use the Halti.

Now your dog behaves without any training collar, *OFF-LEAD!*

Drop on Recall

If you would like to expand on the drop-on-recall exercise that was started during the on-leash work, then do the following:

1. Begin with a straight recall on your long lead.

2. The next time you do a come, tell your dog to do a down just before he reaches you.

3. After he goes down, finish the come, and then do a finish. If your dog does not drop immediately, then step toward him, grab the lead next to his collar, and jerk downward as you say "No!"

4. When your dog goes down immediately in front of you while doing the come, gradually increase the distance at which you give him the down command. If at any time he does not drop immediately, go to him and reprimand him firmly.

It helps to have someone stationed behind your dog to step on the lead, simultaneously with your down command, to stop him, thus reinforcing your command.

5. When your dog is performing consistently, then you can do the exercise without a lead.

Putting It All Together

Be certain to practice this exercise in conjunction with others so that your pet does not learn to anticipate your commands. Mix the down on recall with straight come commands, as well as stays and heeling exercises.

Do not expect expertise of your dog for several months. He will soon become reliable after much repetition and consistency. Remember that you and your dog are a team. If you are unclear in your communication or do not back up commands, then your dog will also become casual in his response. Be enthusiastic and consistent, and praise your dog. It will make the whole process more enjoyable for both of you.

As your dog becomes more proficient with his work, you can introduce new behavior patterns into his repertoire. For example, your dog can learn "outside," "inside," or tricks. I have taught my dogs to return to my vehicle from a distance by using the command "inside." This is handy when traveling or doing a training demonstration. Once you and your pet have accomplished the basics, then you can go on to showing in obedience trials, tracking, or doing performances.

If you would like your dog to do a special job, then I recommend that you consult a professional dog trainer. There are specific training steps that need to be followed in order to achieve success in teaching every new behavior to your dog. Unless you break down the procedures and approach them step by step as each step is successfully mastered, then the whole process can backfire on you. You must also keep in mind that not every dog can perform every job. Each breed of dog was bred for a specific purpose. For example, do not expect a Maltese to be able to track or a Basset Hound to be able to jump high.

Utilizing Your Dog's Natural Instincts

If you want to teach your dog to be protective of your home and family, you needn't go through guard dog training to achieve this. Most dogs are naturally protective of their territory and family pack. Simply praise your dog when he alerts you and barks in a specific situation, and give him the stop command if he barks at the wrong time. Attack training may ruin your dog's personality. Most of the training entails agitating your dog into aggression. This can make him unhappy, nervous, and unpredictable. If you have children this can be extremely dangerous. A child can accidentally give your dog a signal to attack and not know how to turn him off.

As with children, you should give your dog something to occupy his time when alone. Dogs are much happier when working and will stay out of trouble. If you have encouraged your dog to protect your property, then he can be assigned this job when you leave, by saying "Watch the house" every time you go out. When you return, praise him—provided there weren't any break-ins. Another job that your dog can do when you are busy is find a hidden object. I call this the "Find It" game. I'll explain how to teach this in the chapter on dog games.

Now that you and your dog can communicate and work together, your lives will be free of stress and full of fun. We all need a purpose in life, and your dog is no different. When you are able to communicate and work together, your pet will feel fulfilled and happy. Keep in mind that you must habitually work him or he will do "bad" things to gain your attention. A training regimen will give him something to look forward to each day and is a very constructive way for you to spend time together.

You now understand each other and will live harmoniously as *Perfect Companions*.

17. Border Training

IF YOU DO NOT HAVE A FENCED YARD, border training will be invaluable. It is always nice to allow your dog more freedom to exercise and protect his territory. You won't have to worry about his welfare when you let him out to play or relieve himself. I do recommend, nevertheless, that you never leave him outside when you are not home, no matter how well he remains within the boundaries. Dog theft is on the increase.

You can begin border-training your puppy even as you do basic obedience. It is simply a matter of backing up your commands. It is helpful to have a leash attached to your pup's collar while he is loose. This will help bring him back to you when you must reprimand. A puppy over three months old has a tendency to explore. Any time he heads out of the yard or into a room in which he is not allowed, say "No!" and step on the lead. Then crouch down and call him, praising him as he comes.

If your dog is older than six months when you begin border training, I highly advise working on basic and off-lead obedience before working on borders. While you are doing your basic training, you can walk him around the borders as you heel, do stays at the edge, and comes to the inside. During his early training, do not let him loose without a lead until he has a full understanding of "Stay!" and "Come!" with distractions.

Starting with the Long Leash

1. Begin your border training by clearly marking the borders. This marking can be any distinction, such as tarmac to grass. Or, if you are in a neighborhood in which one yard runs into another, then stretch a piece of string along the boundary.

2. Put the long leash on your dog.

3. Walk your dog around the borders doing frequent stays and comes toward the inside.

4. After completing the boundary put your dog on break time.

5. Entice him to go over the boundary by throwing toys out, or enlist the aid of a friend with a dog or children to go running in and out of the yard.

6. Each time your dog nears the border, say "No!" and jerk firmly on the lead, bringing him back into the yard.

7. Then give the "Come!" command. When he comes to you and sits, praise him, and then put him on "Break."

8. Repeat this all around the boundary, daily for at least a week.

Making the Transition to Off-Lead

When your dog responds to your "No!" and no longer needs the physical reprimand of a jerk, then it is time to try this without a leash. Do the procedures in the same manner. Remain in the yard with him for the first few weeks in which he is without a lead. Your next step is to leave the yard, or to hide behind something. Keep an eye on your dog. If he goes near the border, say "No!" Immediately come out, and call him. If he exits the yard, go back to using the long leash.

I advise that if your dog is outside alone you should check on him every few minutes. Even the best-trained dogs have lapses. There are some distractions that are simply irresistible.

18. Dog Games

THERE ARE MANY extracurricular activities in which you and your dog can become involved. You can use each one as a good learning experience, as well as in other ways. For example, playing a game of fetch can teach your dog to retrieve in an obedience trial. On the other hand, teaching your pet to find a hidden toy can be useful in training him to track. These are games in which you and your dog spend quality time together, playing and learning.

Teaching your dog simple tricks will also increase his enthusiasm for work. After he has completed basic obedience, you can teach him to roll over, sit up, speak, lift his paw, or jump over objects.

In this chapter I will discuss the procedures for training your dog to fetch, find, and jump over objects, and to do tricks such as those described above. Practice these along with your normal obedience routine, to break up the monotony.

Retrieve

If your dog is not a natural retriever, this can be a very difficult exercise to teach. I will begin with the procedures for training a puppy, for this is the best time to begin encouraging the retrieve.

Most puppies are natural retrievers. They will pick up, run after, and carry around toy bones, sticks, and balls. When your puppy gets a toy and carries it with his head and tail high, he is indicating that he feels as if he has accomplished quite a feat. Be sure that you praise him to encourage his enthusiasm. If he brings the toy to you, then he should receive lots of praise, for he is presenting you with a gift. Take the toy from him, if he gives it up willingly. Do not wrestle it from his mouth. Wait until he either lays it at your feet or drops it into your hand. Most pups will quickly learn that in order for you to throw it for them they must first give it up.

When you throw the toy for the first time, do not throw it far away. Make sure that your puppy can retrieve it easily. If he chooses to go and play with the toy before bringing it to you, let him play. Do not force the situation. When he presents you with the toy, then you can once again take it and throw it. Always praise him every step of the way.

Some puppies may become particular as to which object they prefer to retrieve. Begin by using only that object until your puupy is very reliable about returning it. Then begin with another toy by using it to play with your puppy. Once you have his attention on the toy, throw it a short distance. If he does not return with it, do not become disconcerted; go back to throwing the one he is good with and intermix the other object into the playtime. Eventually he will return with the other toy, and then you are on your way to his being dependable for retrieving almost anything.

As you play fetch with your puppy, begin to use a command such as "Get it" or "Take it," every time you throw the toy. When your puppy returns to you with the toy, say "Good Dog," and then "Drop." As soon as you have the toy in your hand, praise him again.

If you begin using a word with your fetch command, such as "Get the *ball*" or "Get the *stick*," then your pup will begin to learn object discrimination and the names of things. Soon you can have him fetching whatever object you choose.

If you have an older dog that does not understand the concept of retrieve, then you must go about teaching this behavior in a more methodical manner. We begin with the take-hold-drop.

1. Begin by having your dog sit in the heel position at your left side.

2. Place your left hand over his nose and push his lips into his mouth with your fingers, as you place the object in his mouth with your right hand and say "Take."

3. As soon as the object is in his mouth, praise him and say "Drop" as you let him drop the object from his mouth.

4. As soon as the dog has released the object, give him a treat and praise him.

5. Repeat this procedure four or five times. Then go on to another exercise.

During the next training session you can begin to use the hold command.

1. Begin with your dog in the heel position as you remain standing.

2. Do the take exercise.

3. As soon as the object is in your dog's mouth, hold it shut with your right hand as you say "Hold." Do this very briefly, and then let go as you say "Drop."

Open your dog's mouth with your left hand, as you place the dumbbell in with your right hand. Allow the dumbbell to rest just behind the dog's incisor teeth.

The hold. Hold the dog's mouth shut with the dumbbell inside, as you command "Hold!" Praise your dog the entire time the dumbbell is in his mouth. Begin with only a few seconds of hold. Gradually build on the time the dumbbell rests in the dog's mouth.

4. As soon as your dog drops the object, give him a treat and praise him.

5. The next time you do this, keep the object in your dog's mouth for several seconds longer. Always praise him as he holds the object.

6. Do not do this more than four times in succession. Try to work it in between exercises in which your dog is already accomplished.

7. When your dog is holding the object with your hand around his mouth without objection—isn't trying to get away from you or whining—then you can begin to release your hand pressure around his mouth. If he begins to drop the object as you release the pressure, say "No!" and reapply the pressure.

8. Always praise him as long as the object is in his mouth, and also after you have said "Drop" and he releases the object.

Be Patient! It Takes Time

It can sometimes take weeks for a dog to finally hold the object without your hand having to be around his mouth. Be patient, and always make sure that he is successful. Once he will hold an object in his mouth for about thirty seconds without your having to reprimand him for dropping it—

before you give the command to do so—then it is time to teach him to take it without your having to put it in his mouth.

I have found that putting a bit of cheese on the object is helpful. The cheese makes it more tempting to fetch. This will also prevent your having to force-train your pet any further.

1. Rub some cheese on the object, hold the object directly in front of your dog's nose, and say "Take."

2. Your dog's first reaction will be to sniff and lick the cheese on the object. While he is licking the cheese, slip the object into his open mouth.

3. Praise him, and tell him "Drop."

4. As soon as he drops the object give him a treat and praise.

5. The next time you slip it into his mouth incorporate the "Hold" command.

6. As your dog begins to voluntarily go for the object, begin to move it farther and farther from him before giving him the "Take" command.

7. When he will go for it at an arm's length, then begin gradually lowering the object to the floor in increments, with each successful "Take."

The take. Place the dumbbell directly in front of your dog's mouth, allowing him to sniff it. Holding a treat in the left hand gets the dog interested in the dumbbell.

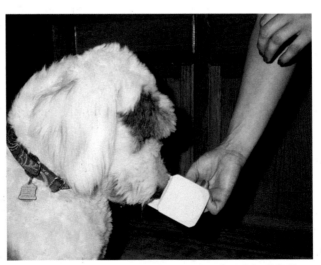

The drop. Allow the dog to let the dumbbell fall as you command "Drop!" Give the dog a treat after a successful take-hold-drop combination.

Putting It Together

Remember that this may take a few days to a few weeks to accomplish, so do not become frustrated or impatient. Eventually the little light bulb in your dog's head will light up!

As your pet becomes reliable in retrieving the object from the floor in front of him, begin to move it farther away with each successive exercise.

When he is retrieving an object from as much as six feet, you can begin to turn it into a playtime routine, or "dog game."

You can either stay put after throwing it or run after it as if you are trying to get it before your dog. This bit of competition usually acts as an incentive for your pet. Another variation on this game is to play tug with the object in between each throw. This further excites the dog into retrieving. Be sure, if you play this tug-and-retrieve game, that your dog drops the object when you command him to do so.

If he maintains a hold on the object after your "Drop!" command, then place your hand over his nose and stick your fingers into his lips. As you apply pressure on his lips (which will push them into his teeth), again say "Drop!" Your dog should drop the object. Be sure to praise him when he drops it, and return to the dog game.

Fly-ball is a dog game that has recently become very popular. There are ways of making special throwing machines that spit out balls for a dog to catch in the air. This is a variation on Frisbee catching. In either game the objective is for the dog to catch the object in the air before it falls. I would recommend teaching your dog fly-ball before working on Frisbee catching, for it is far easier for a dog to grab a ball out of the air than a Frisbee. In either case begin with the following procedures:

1. Place your dog in a sit/stay facing you, not more than six feet away.

2. As you throw the ball, give him your retrieve command.

3. If he catches the ball, praise him; if not, then hold the ball over his head and tease him with it until he jumps up for it. As soon as he is holding it in his mouth, praise him.

4. The next several throws should be from this short distance, until your dog is fully able to catch the ball on every throw.

5. Gradually increase your distance as he develops his catching expertise.

Learning to Catch

Once your dog is reliable at a distance, you can teach him to catch the ball as he is running. This will be most useful with Frisbee fetching. You can do this either by teaching him the "Go-Out"—an advanced obedience behavior that would be described in a book that focuses on utility training— or by pretending to throw the ball in a certain direction but not actually throwing it until he is in motion toward that direction.

For teaching your dog to catch a Frisbee, there are certain steps you must take to ensure that he learns to catch a disk-shaped object.

1. Begin by teaching him to fetch the Frisbee as you roll it on the floor. If he is not interested at first, you may be able to develop his attention by playing tug-of-war with it.

2. When your pet is attracted to the Frisbee, try to roll it along the floor and use your retrieve command.

3. When he is catching it in action (i.e., as the Frisbee is rolling), it is time to try a short distance throw.

4. Gradually increase the height and distance of the throw with each successful retrieve. Be careful not to rush ahead of your pet's ability, or you may find that he quickly loses interest and is turned off the game.

Find It

Another fun dog game that can occupy your dog for several minutes—as well as not involve you directly the whole time—is the "Find It" game. Not only is this activity very enjoyable for your dog, it also begins to instill techniques that are used in tracking and hunting. First, however, your dog must know how to retrieve.

If you teach your dog the names of different toys by consistently using the word as you play with him, he will learn to find any toy you designate. For example, you can hide his ball, and tell him to find his ball. He will continue looking until it is in his mouth. When he returns with it, praise him. Be sure to build on this exercise gradually, as you would with any other procedure.

1. Start by throwing the object a short distance.

2. Gradually increase the distance your dog must go to retrieve it.

3. When your pet is proficient at retrieving, then hide the object in an easy place.

4. Gradually increase the obstacles your dog must overcome to find it.

I have seen dogs searching for up to ten minutes and enjoying themselves thoroughly. A dog is very proud when he finally finds the toy, and returns holding it up high, sometimes prancing back and forth.

Begin by choosing your pet's favorite toy. It must be one he can hardly keep his mouth off. While he is in a sit/stay, place the toy beside a piece of furniture, or, if outside, near a bush, in plain sight. Return to him, release him from his stay, and say "Find it!" He will immediately go to the toy and retrieve it.

When he returns it to you, praise him, and repeat the exercise. Be sure that each time you place the toy you make it more difficult for him to retrieve it. For example, the second time, put it slightly behind another object. The third time, place it completely out of sight. Keep in mind that up to this point your dog is watching where you place it. Once he is very good at retrieving it from out of sight, you can put him in another place so that he cannot see you hide it. When you allow him back in the room or outdoor area, tell him to find it. This is where the real excitement begins.

Your dog will use his tracking abilities to pick up the scent of the toy. Some dogs will be very quick about finding the toy wherever it is hidden, and others will go on looking for a long time because they are predominantly using their sight to find it. The dog that finds the toy quickly is likely to be a good tracking and hunting dog.

If your dog does not have a favorite toy, you can use a treat. This will also help with the dog that is not using scent to find the toy. He will begin to use his nose when there is food to be found.

Roughhousing

Many people like to roughhouse with their dogs. This can also be considered a dog game, but it must be done in the appropriate manner. There are a few dos and don'ts to consider.

I will begin with an explanation of the don'ts. As you have learned by now, you should never let your dog show any type of dominance over you. This is especially so when playing with your pet. Dogs learn through play at a very young age. If they are not disciplined when doing something that will be unacceptable later in life, then the behavior not only persists but becomes more domineering. For example, if you let your puppy bite you in play, he will also bite you when he wants to show you who is in charge. If you reprimand your puppy immediately when he puts his mouth on you by doing an alpha shake or rollover, then he will learn to be more careful and respect you.

Another behavior of which you should be aware is any response of aggression, such as a low growling or showing of the sides of the teeth. Some puppies get carried away with their play, dominance behavior and do not know when to turn it off. You must put a stop to these reactions in the same quick manner you would use when the puppy puts his mouth on you.

The best way to roughhouse with your dog is on *your* terms. Begin on the floor at your dog's level. He will be most likely to become playful if he doesn't feel submissive. While on the floor push at him gently and grab his forelegs. Another way of inviting him to play is to assume the "Play Invite" position: on all fours with your front end down and your back end up.

Roughhousing. You can get on the floor and play with your dog without allowing him to bite or jump on you. You can push him over, gently grab and pull his legs, and give him lots of hugs.

Tapping the floor with your hands while in this position can further excite your dog. Tumbling around on the floor with him as you grab his legs, let go, and fall on your back will keep the game under control but still allow for you both to have fun.

Tricks

Something most dogs enjoy is learning tricks—the kind *you* want them to do. I often intersperse a training lesson with the teaching of tricks, especially if I see a dog that is lagging or showing other signs of inattentiveness. Dogs enjoy learning new things, especially if it involves getting treats or extra praise. Most of the tricks are easiest if your dog has already learned some basic obedience, such as rolling over, barking on command, and sitting up. A trick such as shaking (or lifting a paw) is easier when your dog already knows how to do a sit/stay. The basic obedience training is also helpful in teaching him that he cannot become excessive in these new tricks, such as pawing at you for attention or barking excessively.

Shaking
This behavior is taught with "operant conditioning" in gradual increments.

The shake. When you hold a treat in your left hand, the dog has to move its head to accept the treat as you give the verbal "Shake!" command. Hold your right hand up to receive a paw as it is lifted––when your dog goes for the treat.

Sparky, a three-month-old Jack Russell Terrier, learning to shake.

1. Place your dog in a sit/stay.

2. Put your hand on his foreleg and give him a command such as "Paw" or "Shake."

3. Lift his paw and praise him. If you wish, you can also give him a treat.

4. Repeat this gesture four or five times, and then go on to something that your dog already knows how to do.

5. When you return to this trick, begin by giving the command but not lifting the paw. Touch the dog's shoulder, lightly shoving him so you lift his weight from the side of the paw you are requesting. If he lifts the paw, praise him; if not, keep touching a little more firmly until he moves it by accident. Then praise him.

6. Gradually increase your requirement with each "Paw" or "Shake" command. Make your dog lift his foreleg higher each time before you offer him praise and give him a treat.

One of the variations on this paw-shaking behavior is to teach him to distinguish between his right and left side. Simply use the word *right* or *left* in front of the command and urge him to lift the paw you desire. Always praise him for each successive correct behavior and gradually build on it.

Rollover

This is most successful with a dog that has already learned to do the down/stay. It is a simple matter of baiting your pet with food to make his body follow his head.

1. Place your dog in a down/stay.

2. Put some food directly under his nose.

The rollover. Your dog's body will follow the treat when its head can no longer reach it. When your dog completes the roll, give him the treat.

The rollover. Place your dog in a down. With the treat direct your dog's head over his shoulder and back as you give the rollover command.

3. As your pet becomes interested in the food, begin to make his head follow your hand as you bring it over his back.

4. When the food is over your dog's back, following it he will adjust his position to his side. As he does this, give him a command such as "Roll!" or "Over!"

5. As he does that, bring the food over to the side he is lying on.

6. If he tries to bring his head to the food from the opposite direction, then bring your hand back to his other side, and gently push his body over in the direction of the food. When he has rolled onto his other side, then give him praise and the treat.

7. The next time, your dog will most likely follow the food and roll on his own, without your help. If this happens, be sure to praise him, but do not give him the treat until he sits up. Then you have a complete rollover.

8. Your dog will get faster with each successive roll, and soon you will not need to bait him with the food but simply reward him with it when he completes the behavior.

The visual cue for the rollover will be your hand moving in a spiral pointing down. As with all visual cues, you can rapidly reduce this cue once the behavior has set in. For example, you will go from moving your whole body with the signal to only moving your finger.

Speak

This can be tricky if your dog is not prone to barking anyway. Some dogs will begin barking if they hear a certain noise, such as another dog barking, or see something in particular. Most dogs have some specific cue that will set them off. The problem will be learning what this cue is and building on it, then transferring that cue to simply pointing to your ear.

1. Place your dog in a sit/stay.

2. Stand directly in front of him and hold either a treat or his favorite toy over his head.

3. You will need to tease him with the object. Use an enthusiastic voice and say, "What is it?" or whichever command you wish to use to get your dog to speak.

4. When your dog begins to move his mouth or get excited, praise him and give him the toy or treat.

5. The next time, do not give him the treat or toy until he shows either more excitement or moves his mouth more times.

6. Keep building on each previous behavior with each "What is it?" or "Speak" command.

7. Within a short period of time your dog will catch on to what you desire and will actually make a sound on your command.

8. Be sure to praise him very vigorously when he does make noise. Continue to build on the behavior by expecting either more barks or by working on different types of bark in response to different visual cues. For example, teach your dog to bark once if he sees your right hand go to your right ear, or to bark twice if he sees your left hand go to your left ear. You do this by trial and error, and by reinforcing the correct behavior with praise and reward.

Sit-up (Beg)

Your dog can only learn this trick if he has the proper conformational structure, allowing him to balance on his haunches. For example, it can be difficult for a long-bodied dog with short legs, such as a Basset Hound, but easy for a more squarely built dog, such as a Spaniel. There are, however, always some exceptions to the rule, so sometimes it's worth a try just to find out.

1. Begin with your dog in a sit/stay.

2. Stand in front of him.

3. Hold a treat directly over his head.

4. As he starts to reach for the treat, hold it slightly up, out of his reach.

5. When he lifts one paw off the ground, give him the treat.

The sit-up. First place your dog in a sit/stay. Place the treat between your thumb and middle finger, allowing your forefinger to give a visual cue as you give a verbal command. The treat must remain near your dog's nose, or he will jump up for it.

6. The next time, give him support while luring him upward by lifting his forepaw up higher, so that his other paw is also raised up.

7. Each time he does these things, give him the treat.

8. When he becomes confident about sitting up while using your hand to support himself, begin to reduce the amount of pressure that you allow him to put on your hand. You can accomplish this by continuing to lure his head up with the treat at the same time you draw your hand away from him.

9. If he shows signs of going over backward due to an unstable balance, go back to aiding him for a while as he sits up. You will know it is time to reduce your aid when he can sit up without leaning on you.

Jumping up. Hold the treat up in the air, as you coax your dog to get it. You give the treat when your dog returns to the ground, preventing your fingers from being accidentally nipped.

Jumping over Hurdles

Another game that your dog will thoroughly enjoy is jumping over objects. This activity can include going over hurdles, over people, and over other dogs. The best place to begin is with going over different types of hurdle.

Before you begin teaching your dog these new tricks, you must be certain that he is completely grown. I recommend this because a growing dog can be easily injured by jarring himself while jumping. This can lead to permanent injury. It is best, therefore, to begin this procedure only with an adult dog.

1. Begin with a hurdle that is low enough for your dog to walk over.

2. Put the long lead on him.

3. Heel over the hurdle from both directions until your dog is comfortable going over the jump.

4. Place your dog in a sit/stay on one side of the hurdle and walk to the other side, remaining close to the jump.

5. Call your dog to you. As he nears the jump, say "Over" or "Jump."

6. As he nears the jump, begin walking backward, gathering the lead as you do so.

7. After he clears the hurdle, let him approach and sit facing you. Be sure to praise him.

8. Continue to work in this manner for a few training sessions. When your dog is coming over the hurdle without your having to guide him with the lead, then you can perform this exercise without the lead.

9. Be sure to remain near the far side of the hurdle as you call your dog. Then, back up as you give him the "Over" command, stop, and allow him to sit, facing you.

10. When he is reliable in this exercise, you can begin to raise the jumps in gradual increments. I recommend that you do so at one- to two-inch intervals. But be careful never to set the jump higher than one and a half times your dog's own height.

Then guide him over the jump after you call him to you.

Put your dog in a sit/stay on one side of the jump, and walk to the other side.

Jumping Through Hoops

You can do this same procedure using hoops. I have always used a regular hula hoop. I simply place my dog in a sit/stay, holding the hoop in front of me while holding food in my other hand, opposite the dog, as I say "Come Through." You can also do this in combination with two dogs, if the dogs are small enough to fit through the hoop at the same time.

Another variation on this exercise is teaching your dog to retrieve an object on the other side of the jump. You would be combining two tricks in this exercise; so be sure that your dog is reliable in both of them before doing the following:

1. Begin with a low hurdle, and have your dog sit in the heel position at your left side. Position yourself within two feet of the hurdle in front of you.

2. Command your dog to retrieve the object as you throw it over the jump.

3. As your dog nears the jump, give him the "Over" command.

4. When he picks up the object, praise him, and stand just on the opposite side of the jump as you coax him back to you.

5. As he nears the jump with the object in his mouth, once again give him the "Over" command.

6. Praise him enthusiastically as he returns to you with the object and sits in front of you.

If your dog did not go to retrieve the object, or did not go over the jump after the object, then return to working on these exercises separately. If he did not return over the jump with the object in his mouth, then try to do this exercise on a long lead and guide him over.

The jump over. Place one dog or a person in a down position. Using a treat, guide the other dog over the prone dog or person, as you say "Over." Give the jumping dog a treat after each successful jump. If you are using another dog, give it a treat also. If you are using a person, a thank-you should suffice.

7. After several successful repetitions you can begin to increase the height of the jump. Do this very gradually, and be sure that your pet is fully comfortable with the previous setting before increasing the height.

If You Are Still Having Trouble

If you have problems with this exercise, then I recommend that you consult books that may specifically help you to train your dog for OPEN COMPETITION or for COMPANION DOG EXCELLENT showing. These books should cover this exercise as well as many others in greater detail, and may help you overcome any difficulties.

Jumping over Another Dog

The next jumping trick is for your dog to jump over another dog. You must begin, of course, with a dog that is already very well trained in the down and sit/stay. The "jumping dog" also must be used to jumping any sort of hurdle or object comfortably from either side.

1. Begin with one dog in the down/stay.

2. Place your other dog in a sit/stay on one side of the dog in the down/stay.

3. Call the "jumping dog" to you while you are standing on the other side of the dog in the down/stay.

4. If you stand very close to the "down dog" and back up as the "jumping dog" goes over, then the exercise will be successful. If the "jumping dog" should go around the "down dog," then return to working the "jumping dog" over objects about the size of the "down dog." If the "down dog" gets up when you cue the "jumping dog," then you will need to reinforce the distraction-proofing of the "down dog" as he works.

When you are successful with getting each dog to perform his appointed task, then you can begin working on teaching the "jumping dog" to perform the exercise with a visual signal other than yourself on the other side of the "down dog." You can do this with treats.

1. Place each dog in his position.

2. Stand in front of the "down dog."

3. Let the "jumping dog" see the food in the hand opposite where he is sitting.

4. As you give the "Over" command to the "jumping dog," wave the hand with the treats in the direction of the other side of the "down dog." Your "jumping dog" will follow the hand motion and jump over the "down dog." Make sure that the "jumping dog" sits before you give him his treat. Also, don't forget to give a special treat and praise to your "down dog" for his part in the exercise.

When each dog is comfortable with its part, you can begin to build on this exercise. You can teach the "jumping dog" to go over the "down dog" several times in succession before receiving the treat, or you can teach the "jumping dog" to go over the other dog while it is in a sit, in a stand, or moving. It is very impressive to see a couple of dogs performing this routine while doing a come.

Jumping over *You!*

Teaching your dog to jump over *yourself* is probably the most difficult of the jumping tricks. It is best if you can get someone to help you. If you have a helper, then the procedures are exactly the same as the one that you used for teaching your dog to jump over another dog. However, if you cannot always rely on consistent help, then it is also good to know how to do this by yourself.

1. Place your dog in a sit/stay.

2. Lie down in front of your dog while holding a treat in the hand opposite from where he is sitting. For example, if he is sitting at your right side, hold the treat in your left hand. Let him know that there is a treat in your hand.

3. Place your left hand in front of his face and let him sniff the food.

4. As you draw your hand back to your left side, tell him "Over," and be still as he goes over you to obtain the treat in your hand. He may be a little tentative at first about going over you, but if you encourage him he will catch on.

5. When your dog is confident about jumping over you as you lie down, then it is time to begin raising yourself off the floor. Begin by placing yourself in a crouch position (legs and arms underneath your belly, and back up). This will make a higher object for your dog to jump over.

6. When you are in place in front of your dog, as he remains in a sit/stay, then give him the "Over" command, and show him the treat in the hand opposite where he is sitting. If your dog goes around you, then go back to lying on the floor and making him more reliable. If he goes over you, then give him lots of enthusiastic praise and the treat.

You can gradually raise yourself farther and farther off the floor, as you work on getting your dog to jump over you. You must keep in mind, however, that he will only be capable of what his body structure permits. For example, don't expect a Shih Tzu to be able to jump over you while you are on all fours with your belly off the ground. A Springer Spaniel or Golden Retriever would be more likely to accomplish this.

Shaking with two-year-old Choco, an Australian Shepherd.

Matching Your Dog's Natural Abilities to the Task

The dog games I have discussed should bring both you and your pet many hours of enjoyment. Please keep in mind, however, that not every dog will be able to learn all of these tricks.

Different breeds are capable of doing different things. For example, a Retriever is more prone to fetching and holding objects. Also, an Australian Shepherd and a Border Collie are, by nature, more capable of catching a Frisbee in flight.

Be content with your dog's abilities, and above all make this a fun time.

Sydney sits as he should following the recall.

Index